German Battlecruisers 1914–18

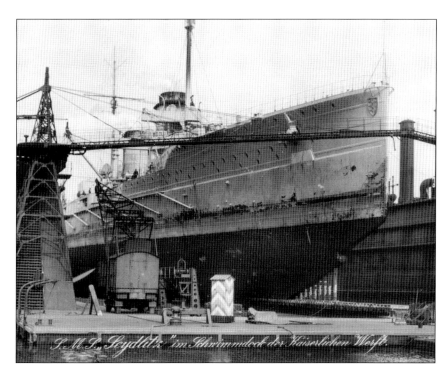

S.M.S. Seydlitz "im Schwimmdock der Kaiserlichen Werft"

Gary Staff • Illustrated by Tony Bryan

First published in Great Britain in 2006 by Osprey Publishing,
Midland House, West Way, Botley, Oxford OX2 0PH, UK
443 Park Avenue South, New York, NY 10016, USA
E-mail: info@ospreypublishing.com

© 2006 Osprey Publishing Ltd

All rights reserved. Apart from any fair dealing for the purpose of private study,
research, criticism or review, as permitted under the Copyright, Designs and
Patents Act, 1988, no part of this publication may be reproduced, stored in
a retrieval system, or transmitted in any form or by any means, electronic,
electrical, chemical, mechanical, optical, photocopying, recording or otherwise,
without the prior written permission of the copyright owner. Enquiries should
be addressed to the Publishers.

A CIP catalogue record for this book is available from the British Library

ISBN 10: 1-84603-009-9
ISBN 13: 978-1-84603-009-3

Page layout by Melissa Orrom Swan, Oxford, UK
Index by Alan Thatcher
Typeset in Helvetica Neue and ITC New Baskerville
Originated by The Electronic Page Company, UK
Printed in China through World Print Ltd

06 07 08 09 10   10 9 8 7 6 5 4 3 2 1

For a catalogue of all books published by Osprey Military and Aviation
please contact:

NORTH AMERICA
Osprey Direct, c/o Random House Distribution Center, 400 Hahn Road,
Westminster, MD 21157
E-mail: info@ospreydirect.com

ALL OTHER REGIONS
Osprey Direct UK, P.O. Box 140 Wellingborough, Northants, NN8 2FA, UK
E-mail: info@ospreydirect.co.uk

www.ospreypublishing.com

Author's acknowledgements

I would like to express my special thanks to the two men without whom this
volume would not have been possible. Mr Stuart Haller has provided numerous
photographs and also many detailed damage reports and much history in
regard to the *Panzerkreuzer* SMS *Seydlitz*. Likewise Mr Carsten Steinhorst
has given many photographs and invaluable drawings and reports about SMS
Lützow. Both these men are experts in their chosen fields and I am indebted
for their help and encouragement. I would also like to thank the staff at the
Bundesarchiv/Militärarchiv for their help and assistance over the years.

Editor's note

Unless otherwise stated all photographs are taken from the author's collection.

GERMAN BATTLECRUISERS 1914–18

INTRODUCTION

The German concept of the battlecruiser was different to that of the British. While the progression and development of the armoured cruiser type had continued in the German Imperial Navy, with regular increases in displacement and armament from *Yorck* (9,530 tonnes), *Scharnhorst* (11,600 tonnes) and finally *Blücher* (15,840 tonnes), the design of the British *Invincible* had taken all by surprise. The path towards the battlecruiser type had been foreseen: in January 1904 Kaiser Wilhelm II had contributed an article to the magazine *Marine-Rundschau* commenting about the narrowing gap between battleship and armoured cruiser displacements. He was critical of the growth in size of armoured cruisers and of their cost and warned that they were not the decisive arbiter of naval battle. However, he realized that because of Germany's numerical inferiority there was a need for the armoured cruisers to be powerfully armed, enabling them to engage the enemy reconnaissance forces successfully. The emperor agreed with the opinion of the State Secretary, Großadmiral von Tirpitz, that the armoured cruisers should continue to be termed large cruisers, or *Großen Kreuzer*. Yet unlike Tirpitz he believed they should be able to be incorporated into the battle line when the battle began, again because of the navy's numerical inferiority. Therefore he believed these ships should take on the characteristics of fast battleships, even if they were still called large cruisers. The Kaiser maintained this opinion in favour of the fast battleship throughout the pre-war period.

Progressional development had continued with the cruiser of 1906, ship E, *Blücher*. However, just one week after the final decision was taken regarding this construction, news arrived from the naval attaché in London that the new British battlecruisers would be armed with

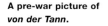

A pre-war picture of *von der Tann*.

SMS *von der Tann* on trials. The four propellers create a powerful suction ahead of themselves, manifested as the low water halfway along the hull. When completed *von der Tann* was the fastest dreadnought warship in the world.

12in calibre guns. This news came at the worst conceivable moment. The jump to dreadnought types the previous year had caused a vast increase in naval costs and Tirpitz was still endeavouring to incorporate this increase into the budget. Now the process was to be repeated with the large cruisers. The *Reichs Marine Amt* (RMA), or Navy Office, immediately recognized that the cruiser of 1906 was inferior in armament, and her defensive capabilities were inadequate against 12in cannon. However, work had already progressed too far, and there were insufficient funds remaining for that financial year to change the design of *Blücher*.

The next large cruiser, the new-build *F* of 1907, was to be a completely new design and the first German battlecruiser, *von der Tann*. This new design had many problems to overcome. The political and financial consequences of the dreadnought type were considerably stretching the available resources. The new design of the *Nassau* class battleships was fully occupying the General Navy Department (A) of the RMA, and the Imperial Dockyards in Kiel, Wilhelmshaven and Danzig were overloaded with new work.

The task of the new *Große Kreuzer* (the term *Schlachtkreuzer* did not come into use in Germany until after the war) was envisaged as the forming of an independent reconnaissance division, able to perform special tasks. They would have a speed superiority of at least 3 knots and should be capable of fighting in the line. Therefore they would require heavy armour and good defensive qualities. State Secretary von Tirpitz was opposed to this line capability.

In July 1906 a representative from the Information Agency of the RMA (N), Korvettenkapitän Vollerthun, wrote a short paper in which he said the newest Royal Navy armoured cruisers did not possess the qualities necessary for fighting in the line. He stated that the armoured cruiser type had not reached its full potential displacement or combat capability and that eventually the battleship and battlecruiser would evolve into a universal common type.

CRUISER *F – VON DER TANN*

The design of *von der Tann* began in August 1906 and continued until June 1907. During this time many proposals and design options were suggested and discussed. All were for heavy armament, and 30.5cm and 34.3cm main guns were considered. However, financial constraints determined that there had to be a balance between armour, engines and armament. A speed increase would come at the cost of a reduction in the number and calibre of the cannon, or both, or a reduction in armour. At a meeting in September 1906 Admiral von Heeringen again stated that the large cruiser should be capable of employment against the enemy battle line. Tirpitz was fundamentally still opposed to this view, and believed the type should only be used against enemy cruisers. Finally it was determined to use the new 28cm double turret with a rate of fire of three rounds per minute. Furthermore, cruiser *F* would be the first German large warship to utilize turbine propulsion. On 22 June 1907 the Kaiser approved the building order for cruiser *F, von der Tann*.

VON DER TANN – SPECIFICATIONS

Building dockyard:	Blohm & Voss
Contract:	26 September 1907
Building number:	198
Keel laying:	21 March 1908
Launch:	20 March 1909
Commissioned:	1 September 1910
Displacement:	Designed: 19,370 tonnes
	Loaded: 21,300 tonnes
Length:	171.7m
Beam:	26.6m
Draught:	Construction: 8.91m
	Loaded: 9.17m
Moulded depth:	13.28m
Performance:	Designed: 42,000shp
	Maximum: 79,802shp
Revolutions per minute:	Designed: 300
	Maximum: 339
Speed:	Designed: 24.8 knots
	Maximum attained: 27.75 knots
Fuel:	Construction: 1,000 tonnes
	Maximum: 2,600 tonnes
Range:	4,400 nautical miles at 14 knots
Cost:	36.523 million marks
Compartments:	15
Double bottom (as % of length):	75
Crew:	41 officers
	882 men

Armament

It was finally determined that cruiser *F* be armed with 8 x 28cm L/45 SK (quick-firing) cannon, the same as those mounted on the *Nassau* class battleships. The guns were fitted in the Drh.L C/1907 (turntable) mount, which was electrically trained and elevated hydraulically. This turret was the first to be fitted with a rotating working chamber, or reloading chamber, and with an integral rangefinder. The guns could be elevated to a maximum of 20°, which gave a range of 18,900m, and after 1915 this was improved out to 20,400m. The 302kg armour-piercing (AP) shell was propelled by a fore charge and main charge at a muzzle velocity of 875mps. The fore charge came in a silk bag, while in common with all German propellant charges the main charge was enclosed in a brass cartridge. This ammunition system was to have profound consequences when German turrets were hit. A total of 660 28cm shells were carried in four shell rooms, each with 165 projectiles. In common with many

German ships of this period, the positioning of the shell rooms and magazines varied from turret to turret. In A turret the magazine was above the shell room, as with wing B and D turrets, whereas C turret, the aft turret, had the opposite arrangement, with the shell room being above the magazine.

Unlike her British contemporaries, *von der Tann* was equipped with a medium-calibre armament that consisted of 10 x 15cm SK L/45 cannon in MPL C/06 (pivot) mounts. An outfit of 150 high-explosive (HE) and AP shells per gun was carried. Prior to 1915 these 45.3kg shells could be ranged to 13,500m, and after this out to 16,800m. *Von der Tann* also carried an outfit of 16 x 8.8cm SK L/45 cannon to fend off torpedo boats and destroyers. They were mounted in the MPL C/01-06 mount and could fire their 9kg shells at an excellent rate of fire of 15 rounds per minute out to an outstanding range of 10,694m. A total of 3,200 rounds were carried for these guns.

Finally there were 4 x 45cm torpedo tubes: one in the bow, one in the stern and two on the broadside. A total of 11 torpedoes were carried. The 800kg torpedo carried a warhead of 110kg and had a range of 2,000m at 32 knots and 1,500m at 36 knots.

Von der Tann coaling. The device fitted to the guns of C turret is for gunnery training. One barrel was used to move the target at random, and the gun leader of the other gun had to follow these movements with his sighting telescope. The coloured lights on the main mast are for signalling at night time. (Courtesy of Stuart Haller)

Armour

Because of the stated requirement for the *Große Kreuzer* to be capable of fighting in the battle line, the German battlecruisers were much more heavily armoured than their British counterparts. A greater percentage of their weight was allocated to armoured protection, yet without being detrimental to other qualities and requirements.

COMPARISON OF PERCENTAGE OF WEIGHTS IN TONNES		
Ship:	von der Tann	Indefatigable
Hull:	6,004 (31.5%)	7,000 (37.4%)
Machinery:	3,034 (15.9%)	3,655 (19.5%)
Armour & Protection:	5,693 (29.8%)	3,735 (19.9%)
Armament:	2,604 (13.7%)	2,580 (13.8%)

Von der Tann utilized 10 per cent more of her weight for armour and protection than *Indefatigable*, its eventual opponent in the Skagerrak Battle (Jutland). Not only was this weight used to produce thicker armour, it also extended the armour over a far greater area of the ship. The armoured belt extended from the stem to almost the stern and the citadel extended from the upper deck to 1.6m below the waterline. The main belt armour was 80–120mm thick forward, 250mm thick over the citadel, tapering to 225mm at the top, and was 100mm thick aft. The forward conning tower was 250mm and the aft conning tower was 200mm thick. Turrets had 230mm faces, 180mm sides and the roofs were 90mm thick. The horizontal armour consisted of an upper armoured deck of 25mm thickness and a main armoured deck of 25mm. The sloping deck armour (*Böschung*) was 50mm and armoured transverse bulkheads were 120, 140 and 170mm thick.

One advantage that all the German large cruisers from *Blücher* onwards had was an armoured torpedo bulkhead. In the case of *von der Tann* this was 25mm thick. The torpedo bulkhead stretched the length of the citadel, from the bow turret to the aft turret, and was set back a distance of 4m from the hull outer skin. The intervening space was divided in two by a gangway longitudinal bulkhead, the inner section of which was used to store coal. The torpedo bulkhead saved German ships from severe underwater damage on numerous occasions, and although the battlecruisers were damaged by torpedoes or mines six times, they were not destroyed due to this protection. None of the British battlecruisers at the Skagerrak Battle had the protection of a torpedo bulkhead, while the *Iron Duke* class were the first battleships to be provided with one.

Von der Tann's armour was Krupp cemented and nickel steel.

Sea keeping

Von der Tann had a metacentric height of 2.11 metres. (A higher metacentric height gives sharper movements, but increased stability, especially with flooding.) Frahm anti-rolling tanks were fitted during construction, but they were not completely successful as they were located too far inboard. Bilge keels were subsequently fitted to replace them. Nevertheless, *von der Tann* was known to be a fine sea ship with gentle movements. Manoeuvring and steering were good with a speed loss of 60 per cent and an 8° heel with the application of full rudder.

Machinery

Von der Tann had 18 naval double boilers in five divided boiler rooms. As a measure to save weight, the German Navy had developed the double boiler with two steam drums and four water drums. The small tube boilers produced steam at a pressure of 235psi, or 16 atmospheres.

A photograph taken in floating dock shows an armoured plate of *von der Tann* dislodged by the first heavy hit made on her at the Skagerrak Battle. A 15in projectile fired by *Barham* struck *von der Tann* at 1709hrs and resulted in 600 tonnes of water flooding into the ship.

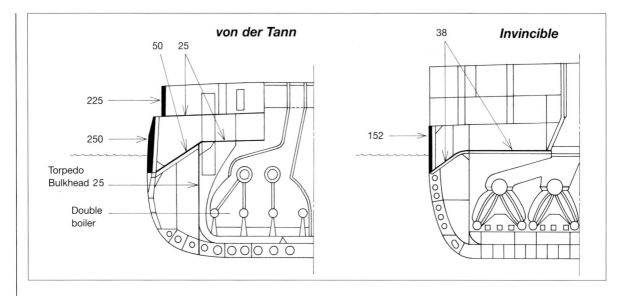

Comparative cross sections of *von der Tann* and *Invincible* (armour thickness given in mm).

Von der Tann was the first large German warship to have turbine propulsion. As with all *Großen Kreuzer*, there were two sets of turbines with the high-pressure turbines working on the outer shafts, and the low-pressure turbines working on the inner shafts. In *von der Tann* the astern turbines were also on the wing shafts. The turbines were made by Parsons and drove four propellers of 3.6m diameter. Designed output was to be 42,000 shaft horse power (shp) at 300rpm for a speed of 24.8 knots. As with all German turbine-driven ships, the turbines could be considerably overloaded and on trials they produced 79,802shp for 339rpm and a maximum speed of 27.75 knots. After 1916 the boiler firing was supplemented by tar-oil firing.

Von der Tann had two parallel rudders that were operated by steam-powered rudder engines. The electrical plant had six steam turbo generators with a total output of 1,200kw.

General characteristics and changes

Von der Tann was originally designed with a lattice mast, but this was not fitted. She was the only large cruiser in which the officers were accommodated forward and the crew mainly aft, and this was not considered a successful arrangement. In late 1914 spotting tops were fitted to the masts for the observation of artillery fire. Anti-torpedo nets were removed in late 1916. The 8.8cm SK cannon were also later removed and their apertures were welded closed, and two 8.8cm Flak cannon replaced those on the aft superstructure. During late 1915 a crane was erected on the aft deck and trials were conducted enshipping a seaplane.

Von der Tann was a very successful ship, and a milestone in the development of German cruisers. Credit must be given to its design team: Department Chief Oberbaurät Hüllmann, Geheim Bauräte Bürkner and Konow, and for the engine plant, Geheim Oberbaurät Veith.

Namesake

Cruiser *F* was named after Freiherr Ludwig von und zu der Tann-Rathsamhausen, who was born in Darmstadt on 18 June 1815 and died on 26 April 1881. He served as a General der Infanterie for the Bavarian forces.

Trials with floatplanes were conducted aboard *von der Tann* in autumn 1915. Here a Friedrichshafen FF29 is hoisted aboard with an improvised derrick aft. (Courtesy of Carsten Steinhorst)

Service record

Commanders:

Kapitän zur See Mischke	September 1910–September 1912
Kapitän zur See Hahn	September 1912–February 1916
Kapitän zur See Zenker	February 1916–April 1917
Kapitän zur See Mommsen	April 1917–July 1918
Kapitän zur See Karl Feldmann	July 1918–December 1918
Kapitänleutnant Wollanke	Internment

On 29 July 1907 the Blohm & Voss dockyard at Hamburg received the contract to construct ship *F*, and the keel was laid on 21 March 1908. On 20 March 1909 the ship was launched and christened *von der Tann* by the nephew of Baron Ludwig. In May 1910 the *von der Tann* departed Hamburg and sailed around the Skagen for final fitting-out in the Imperial Dockyard, Kiel. It is a fact that the Imperial Navy were always short of crews and therefore a dockyard crew conducted the transfer. When on 1 September 1910 *von der Tann* was commissioned, the majority of her crew came from *Rheinland*.

During a six-hour forced trial an average speed of 27 knots was achieved, and with a highest speed of 28.124 knots *von der Tann* was the fastest dreadnought in the world. This performance clearly invalidated the theory that speed must be bought at the expense of protection. Trials in the open sea followed with a voyage to South America departing 20 February 1911. The *Große Kreuzer* visited Rio de Janeiro, Puerto Mitilar and Bahia Blanco. *Von der Tann* returned to Kiel on 6 May 1911 and covered the 1,913 nautical miles from Tenerife to Helgoland at an average speed of 24 knots, a very creditable performance.

On 8 May 1911 *von der Tann* joined the Unit of Reconnaissance Ships and therefore participated in all the unit's exercises and manoeuvres before the outbreak of war. In June 1911 *von der Tann* attended the review at Spithead for the coronation of King George V.

The outbreak of war saw *von der Tann* as flagship of the 3rd Admiral of Reconnaissance Forces, Kontreadmiral Tapken. She participated in the resultless counter-thrust against British forces after the Helgoland Battle. On 2–3 November 1914 she took part in the bombardment of

Great Yarmouth and on 15–16 December 1914 in the bombardment of Scarborough and Whitby. *Von der Tann* suffered no damage in these engagements.

On 25 December 1914 the position of 3rd Admiral was abolished. *Von der Tann* was not present at the Dogger Bank Battle on 24 January 1915 as she was in dockyard hands. On 10 August, however, *von der Tann* attacked the island fortress at Utö in the eastern Baltic and opened fire on the shore batteries, five Russian destroyers and the armoured cruiser *Bayan*. In return she suffered a shell through the forward funnel, but there were no casualties. Further fleet advances into the North Sea followed on 11–12 September, 19–20 October and 23–24 October 1915.

The year 1916 began for *von der Tann* on 3–4 February with the fleet advance to welcome home the raider *Möwe*. Further advances in the Hoofden followed on 5–7 March, to the north on 17 April, and to Horns Reef on 21–22 April and 5 May. *Von der Tann* participated in the bombardment of Lowestoft and Great Yarmouth on 24–25 April 1916.

In the Skagerrak Battle from 31 May to 1 June 1916, *von der Tann* was the last ship in the I Reconnaissance Group (I AG). Highlights of the battle for *von der Tann* were as follows:

1649hrs	*von der Tann* opens fire on *Indefatigable*.
1703hrs	*Indefatigable* explodes after suffering five 28cm shell hits out of 52 projectiles fired by *von der Tann*.
1709hrs	First heavy hit – a 15in shell from *Barham* strikes aft and 600 tonnes of water penetrate the ship.
1723hrs	Second hit – a 13.4in shell from *Tiger* hits near C turret, puts this turret out of action, and affects the starboard rudder engine room.
1750hrs	Protective bunker compartment IVB makes water.
1751hrs	Third heavy hit – a 13.4in shell from *Tiger* strikes A turret and jams it at 120°.
1820hrs	D turret fails, so that no turrets remain in action (B failed previously). Nevertheless Kapitän zur See Zenker holds his place in line to distract the enemy.

The German battlecruisers during the raid on Yarmouth on 3 November 1914. Ahead is *Seydlitz*, then *Moltke*, *Blücher* and *von der Tann*.

Another photograph taken from *von der Tann* shows *Seydlitz*, *Moltke* and *Derfflinger* on the raid against Scarborough and Whitby on 16 December 1915. The faces of *Derfflinger*'s turrets have been painted red as a recognition device.

1853hrs	Speed falls from 26 to 23 knots.
1930hrs	D turret repaired.
2019hrs	Fourth heavy hit – a 15in shell from *Revenge* puts the aft conning tower out of action.
2030hrs	B turret again serviceable.
2100hrs	C turret again clear for action.

Following the action the cruiser had 11 dead and 35 wounded. She was under repair in the Imperial Dockyard, Wilhelmshaven, from 2 June to 29 July. *Von der Tann* then participated in the fleet advances on 18–19 August, 25–26 September, 18–19 October and 23–24 October 1916 and 23–24 March 1917. During this period she twice suffered turbine damage and lay in the dockyard from 13 November 1916 to 29 December 1916 and from 31 May to 22 June 1917.

Von der Tann took part in the advance to Norway on 23–25 April 1918 as flagship of Kontreadmiral von Reuter, and in the advance of 8–9 July. The cruiser was ready for the planned fleet advance on 30 October 1918. *Von der Tann* was interned at Scapa Flow and was scuttled by her crew on 21 June 1919. She was raised on 7 December 1930 and scrapped.

CRUISERS *G* AND *H* – *MOLTKE* AND *GOEBEN*

Even while building preparations were still in progress for *F*, the navy's Construction Department began working on specifications for the cruiser of 1908. At a conference in May 1907 it had already been decided that cruiser *G* should be enlarged.

With an allocation of 44 million marks for the financial year 1908, there was the possibility of following the battleships with an increase to 30.5cm guns. However, up until now the 28cm SK was sufficient, even against foreign battleships. The Construction Department and Tirpitz thought that a quantitive increase was a better tactical option and the numerical inferiority to the British in the cruiser battle was considered sufficient grounds to increase the number of barrels. The armour was to be no less than *F* and the speed no less than 24.5 knots.

Moltke being fitted out in the Blohm & Voss shipyard at Hamburg. (Courtesy of Stuart Haller)

The General Navy Department responded to this by saying that for the cruiser to participate in the line battle a heavier-calibre gun was desired. Nevertheless a conference on 17 May 1907 decided on the 28cm gun in a superfiring arrangement, allowing ten guns on the broadside.

Design work proceeded slowly because of staff shortages and over this period there were many weight increases due to increasing the ammunition outfit, citadel size and armour thickness, and revisions of the boiler system. As the production of single ships was placing a great strain on the various departments of the RMA it was decided to construct *G* and *H* to the same design. Blohm & Voss' low quote for *G* ensured they also received the contract for the cruiser of 1909, *H*.

		Moltke	*Goeben*
Building dockyard:		Blohm & Voss	Blohm & Voss
Contract:		17 September 1908	8 April 1909
Building number:		200	201
Keel laying:		7 December 1908	12 August 1909
Launch:		7 April 1910	28 March 1911
Commissioned:		30 September 1911	2 July 1912
Displacement:	Designed:	22,979 tonnes	22,979 tonnes
	Loaded:	25,400 tonnes	25,400 tonnes
Length:		186.6m	186.6m
Beam:		29.4m	29.4m
Draught:	Construction:	8.77m	8.77m
	Loaded:	9.19m	9.19m
Moulded depth:		14.08m	14.08m
Performance:	Designed:	52,000shp	52,000shp
	Maximum:	85,782shp	85,661shp
Revolutions per minute:	Maximum:	332	330
Speed:	Designed:	25.5 knots	25.5 knots
	Maximum attained:	28.4 knots	28.0 knots
Fuel:	Construction:	1,000 tonnes	1,000 tonnes
	Maximum:	3,100 tonnes	3,100 tonnes
Range:		4,120 nautical miles at 14 knots	4,120 nautical miles at 14 knots
Cost:		42.603 million marks	41.564 million marks
Compartments:		15	15
Double bottom (as % of length):		78	78
Crew:		43 officers	43 officers
		1,010 men	1,010 men

Armament

The main armament was increased to 10 x 28cm SK L/50 cannon. The guns were fitted in Drh.L C/1908 turrets mountings that allowed an elevation of 13.5°, less than in *von der Tann,* and accordingly the range was less at 18,100m. In 1916 the elevation was increased to 16° for a slight improvement to 19,100m. The semi-AP and AP shells both weighed 302kg and were fired at a rate of up to three rounds per minute with a muzzle velocity of 895mps. A total of 810 projectiles were carried in shell rooms, all located on the lower platform deck with the magazines above them on the upper platform deck.

The secondary armament was 12 x 15cm SK L/45 cannon in the MPL C/06 mounts. A total outfit of 1,800 shells were carried – 150 per gun. Initially ranged to 13,500m the range was later increased out to 16,800m. In May 1915 *Goeben* had the No.4 15cm guns demounted and transferred ashore. The *Moltke* and *Goeben* were also designed and fitted with 12 x 8.8cm SK L/45 guns, but these were gradually removed and those on the aft superstructure were replaced with 8.8cm Flak L/45 cannon (*Flugzeug Abwehr Kanone* – Flak). The *Moltke* class carried 4 x 50cm torpedo tubes, mounted below the waterline in the bow and stern, and two on the broadside forward. A total of 11 G/7 model torpedoes were shipped.

A pre-war picture of *Moltke* shows her at full speed and flying the flag of Vizeadmiral Bachmann, Commander of Reconnaissance Forces. *Moltke* achieved a maximum speed of 28.4 knots during her trials.

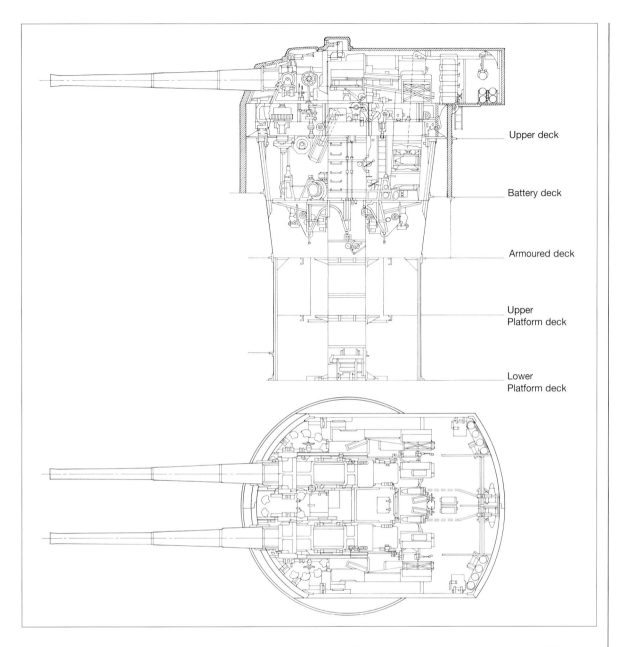

Upper deck

Battery deck

Armoured deck

Upper
Platform deck

Lower
Platform deck

**The Drh.L C/1908 turret and
28cm SK cannon.**

This torpedo weighed 1,365kg with an explosive charge of 195kg and
could range to 9,300m at 27 knots, and 4,000m at 37 knots.

Armour

The armour of this class was increased in thickness. The main belt was
100mm aft, 270mm in the citadel and 100mm forward. The casemate
armour was 150mm with 35mm roofs. The forward conning tower
was 350mm and the aft conning tower was 200mm thick. Turrets had
230mm vertical armour, 180mm sides and the roofs were 90mm thick.
The deck armour totalled 50mm and the sloping armour was also 50mm.
The torpedo bulkhead was 50mm in front of the barbettes, and 30mm
otherwise. As with *von der Tann*, the armour was Krupp cemented and
nickel steel.

Sea keeping

The ships of the *Moltke* class had a metacentric height of 3.01m. They were good sea ships with gentle pitching movements and quiet motion. Going ahead they turned well, but were slow to answer the helm. There was a 60 per cent speed loss and 9° heel with the rudder hard over.

Machinery

The *Moltke* class had 24 naval boilers in four boiler rooms. The boilers reverted to the smaller type with one steam drum and three water drums and were installed three abreast in each of the four boiler rooms. They produced steam at 235psi and after 1916 were fitted with supplemental tar-oil spraying.

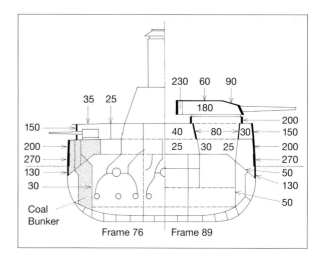

There were two sets of Parsons turbines. The forward and aft engine rooms were each partitioned into three, with the high-pressure turbines on the outer shafts in the forward wing rooms, and the low-pressure turbines on the inner shafts in the larger aft engine room. The shafts drove four propellers of 3.74m diameter. On trials both ships exceeded 28 knots.

Details of armour (given in mm) on *Moltke* and *Goeben*.

The two rudders were fitted in tandem, as the fine lines of the stern precluded parallel rudders. Parallel rudders gave better manoeuvring at slow speed, but tandem allowed for an uninterrupted prop wash. The likelihood of a hit disabling both rudders was reduced and the loss of one rudder would not give asymmetric steering. However, the disadvantage was that there was no direct action of prop wash, so at slow speed the turning circle was greater. On trials the forward rudder proved less effective.

Moltke had six turbo dynamos providing 1,500kw of power at 225 volts.

General characteristics and changes

A cowl was added to *Moltke*'s forward funnel in 1912. *Goeben*'s aft funnel did not have a jacket. Both ships carried spotting tops from 1914. Seaplane trials were conducted aboard *Moltke* in autumn 1915.

Namesake – *Moltke*

Moltke was named after Graf Helmuth von Moltke (1800–91), the Prussian Generalfeldmarschall.

Service record – *Moltke*

Commanders:

Kapitän zur See Ritter von Mann
Edler von Tiechler   September 1911–January 1913
Fregattenkapitän/Kapitän zur See
Magnus von Levetzow   January 1913–January 1916
Kapitän zur See von Karpf   January 1916–September 1916
Kapitän zur See Gygas   September 1916–December 1918
Korvettankapitän Hans Humann
and Korvettankapitän Schirmacher   May 1918–September 1918
Kapitänleutnant Crelinger   Internment

On 7 April 1910 General der Infanterie Helmuth von Moltke christened ship *G*, named after his uncle. On 10 September 1911 a

Moltke about to pass under the Rendsburg High Railway Bridge, sometime during the war. The transit of the Kaiser Wilhelm Canal was always a pleasant experience for the crew as they could stand down from the rigours of keeping a war watch, as they would have to at sea. The ship was under the guidance of a pilot and everyone could relax. (Courtesy of Stuart Haller)

dockyard crew transferred *Moltke* from Hamburg to Kiel via the Skagen, and on 30 September *Moltke* was commissioned and replaced *Roon* in the Reconnaissance Unit. Trials continued until 1 April 1912 and on 19 April 1912 *Moltke* formed part of a cruiser division that sailed for North America, reaching Cape Henry on 30 May. A visit to New York followed before returning to Kiel on 24 June.

A further special task followed in July 1912 when *Moltke* escorted the Kaiser's yacht to Russia. After returning on 9 July, *Moltke* served as flagship of the Commander of Reconnaissance Forces. After this she participated in all the exercises and manoeuvres conducted by the High Sea Fleet.

On 23 June 1914 Kontreadmiral Hipper lowered his flag on *Moltke* and the new cruiser *Seydlitz* became flagship. Thereafter consideration was given to dispatching *Moltke* to East Asia in the autumn to replace *Scharnhorst*, but after the summer cruise to Norway this plan was dropped as now it became necessary for *Moltke* to replace *Goeben* in the Mediterranean. The outbreak of war interrupted this plan.

On 28 August 1914 *Moltke* was one of the cruisers that delivered the resultless counterblow after the Helgoland Battle. She then took part in the advances to the British coast at Great Yarmouth on 2–4 November and Hartlepool on 15–16 1912. Here *Moltke* received a 6in shell hit from the coastal batteries. *Moltke* then took part in the Dogger Bank Battle without sustaining damage, and in the fleet advances on 29–30 March and in April and May.

On 3 August 1915 *Moltke* went to the Baltic with I AG (I Reconnaissance Group) to support the attack on the Riga Gulf by Vizeadmiral Ehrhard Schmidt, and on 19 August *Moltke* fell victim to a torpedo fired by the British submarine *E1*. The torpedo was not sighted until it was just a cable-length (200 yards) away, and it struck the bow torpedo room. Several torpedo heads were rent open but did not detonate. Eight men perished

On 19 August 1915 while in the Baltic Sea, *Moltke* was hit by a torpedo. This photograph shows her in the floating dock at Blohm & Voss, Hamburg on 24 August, just after repair work was commenced. (Courtesy of Stuart Haller)

and 435 tonnes of water flooded into the ship; however, *Moltke* was able to maintain the unit speed of 15 knots. Repairs were carried out at Blohm & Voss, Hamburg from 23 August to 20 September 1915. *Moltke* participated in the fleet advance of 23–24 October and then all subsequent operations up until the end of May 1916.

In the Skagerrak Battle, *Moltke* was the fourth ship in I AG and her shooting was excellent. During the first 12 minutes of battle she hit the British *Tiger* nine times at ranges from 14,300m to 12,300m, and then a further four times in the next 30 minutes. In return *Moltke* was struck four times by 15in shells on:

Starboard No.5 15cm gun (put out of action)
Hull side near stern
Armoured belt below No.2 starboard 15cm casemate
Armoured belt just abaft main mast

Casualties were 16 dead and 20 wounded, mainly due to hit 1. Flooding and counter-flooding caused 1,000 tonnes of water to enter the ship.

Towards 1947hrs Vizeadmiral Hipper quit his flagship *Lützow* to transfer to another ship, and eventually boarded *Moltke* at 2205hrs. After the battle *Moltke* was repaired at Blohm & Voss, Hamburg from 7 June until 30 July, and after training in the Baltic was combat-ready on 14 August 1916.

On 18–20 August *Moltke* led the reinforced I AG during the fleet advance against Sunderland and on 25–26 September supported an advance by small cruisers. Later, on 4 November, she took part in the advance to Bovbjerg to recover *U20* and *U30*, during which *Großer Kurfürst* and *Kronprinz* were torpedoed by submarine *J1*.

In September 1917 *Moltke* transferred to the Baltic as the flagship of Vizeadmiral Ehrhard Schmidt for the operation to capture the Baltic Islands. An army force of 23,000 men and supporting equipment was landed on Ösel Island on 12 October under the protection of *Moltke* and the III and IV Battle Squadrons. In a campaign that lasted until 20 October the German forces carried out the most successful amphibious assault conducted by any belligerent during World War I. German losses were seven minesweepers and 156 naval dead, and 54 army dead. The Russians lost the destroyer *Grom* and battleship *Slava*, and 20,130 prisoners. With the successful conclusion of the operation the Russian flank was turned and the retreat of the Russian fleet opened the way to Reval and the Aaland Islands, which threatened St Petersburg and had great importance for the later liberation of Finland in 1918.

On 3 November *Moltke* was detached to the North Sea and had hardly returned when on 17 November she supported II AG in the second battle of Helgoland, but did not come into action. After this she went into the dockyard until 14 December.

Some crew on the poop deck of *Moltke* as a Zeppelin flies overhead. (Courtesy of Stuart Haller)

On 29 March 1918 *Moltke*, *Hindenburg* and IV AG supported the 14th Torpedoboote Halb Flottille. On 19 April *Moltke*, *Derfflinger* and IV AG supported the III Flottille in their abortive transfer to Flanders.

On 23–24 April 1918 the last large-scale fleet operation took place to interrupt convoy traffic between England and Norway. As I AG stood 60 nautical miles ahead of the main body, just south-west of Bergen, *Moltke* suffered a catastrophe. At around 0610hrs the starboard inner propeller flew off, the turbine over sped and a wheel of the engine turning gear disintegrated. Part of the wheel struck the outlet pipe of the auxiliary condenser, several steam pipes and the deck of the main switchboard room. Because of the auxiliary condenser the middle engine room and the switchboard room filled with water, and the outboard engine room also began to fill. The boilers were salted and therefore the entire engine plant fell out. The ship made 1,600 tonnes of water. Finally a diver succeeded in closing the auxiliary condenser sea valve and the slide gate valve of the inlet and outlet, and the water was at last mastered. At 1038hrs *Straßburg* attempted to take her in tow, but it was only at 1113hrs that *Oldenburg* successfully took up the tow. About 1710hrs the following day the engines were again clear and could deliver a speed of 13 knots, after the cruiser had been towed right across the North Sea. A short time later, at 1937hrs, the submarine *E42* successfully torpedoed *Moltke*. The torpedo struck outside the port, outboard engine room, 1,761 tonnes of water flooded into the ship and speed was reduced to 4 knots. Tugs came to *Moltke*'s assistance and at 0856hrs on 26 April she anchored off Wilhelmshaven, where repairs were carried out in the Imperial Dockyard from 30 April to 9 September 1918.

After further training in the Baltic from 19 September to 3 October, *Moltke* stood ready for the planned fleet operation of 30 October. From 1 November 1918 *Moltke* again served as I AG flagship for Kontreadmiral von Reuter.

Moltke was interned at Scapa Flow and was scuttled on 19 June 1919. She was later raised and scrapped.

Namesake – *Goeben*

Goeben was named after August Karl von Goeben (10 December 1816–13 November 1886), Imperial Prussian General der Infanterie.

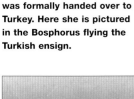

In November 1918, *Goeben* was formally handed over to Turkey. Here she is pictured in the Bosphorus flying the Turkish ensign.

Service record – *Goeben*

Commanders:

Kapitän zur See Phillip	July 1912–April 1914
Kapitän zur See Richard Ackerman	April 1914–January 1918
Kapitän zur See Stoelzel	January 1918–November 1918
Korvettenkapitän Lampe	July 1918–August 1918

At the end of 1908 the contract for the new-building cruiser *H* was let under the appropriations for the budget 1908–09. This event gave rise to the incorrect statement by the British Admiralty that Germany would build naval shipping in excess of that allowed by the Fleet Law (which controlled the size and cost of the German Navy), and led the British parliament to approve ten capital ships in order to keep pace in the 'arms race'.

On 28 March 1911 the new ship was launched and christened by Commanding General of the VIII Armeekorps, General der Infanterie von Ploetz. Trials began in June 1912 and *Goeben* was commissioned on 2 July. The trials were interrupted from 29 August to 24 September as *Goeben* participated in the autumn manoeuvres.

In October 1912 the First Balkan War erupted. The Armee High Command determined that a naval Mediterranean Division was required and to this end *Goeben* and *Breslau* departed Kiel on 4 November. On 15 November they anchored off Constantinople. From April 1913 *Goeben* began visiting the ports of Venice, Pola and Naples and then moved into Albanian waters. She then went to Pola from 21 August to 16 October for repairs. The Second Balkan War, beginning on 29 June 1913, meant there was no thought of dissolving the Mediterranean Division.

On 23 October 1913, Kontreadmiral Souchon became Chief of the Division, and from then until the beginning of World War I *Goeben* continued to show the flag, visiting over 80 destinations. When Archduke Franz Ferdinand was assassinated at Sarajevo Kontreadmiral Souchon recognized the threat of war and immediately went to Pola, where *Goeben* had 4,460 boiler tubes replaced. From there the cruisers went to Messina and on 4 August bombarded the French Algerian ports of Bone and Philippeville. On the return journey to Messina, *Goeben* and *Breslau* were chased by *Indefatigable*, *Indomitable* and *Dublin*, but outran the British ships after a long stern chase. The two cruisers were then ordered to Turkey and, after avoiding a British armoured cruiser force, arrived off the Dardanelles on 10 August. *Breslau* had exchanged fire with *Gloucester*.

The first military operation against Russia followed on 29 October when *Goeben* bombarded Sevastopol. In return fire she was hit by a 10in

A good view of *Seydlitz* travelling at speed before the beginning of the war. (Courtesy of Stuart Haller)

shell in the aft funnel, although the shell failed to detonate. On departing, the Russian minelayer *Prut*, with 700 mines aboard, was captured and sunk, and the Russian destroyer *Leitenant Pushchin* was hit with two 15cm shells. The Russian response was to declare war on Turkey on 1 November, while Britain and France pre-empted their declaration of 5 November with a bombardment of the Dardanelle forts on 3 November. The proposed sale of *Goeben* to Turkey had certainly contributed to bringing Turkey into the war on the side of the Central Powers.

On 18 November *Goeben* encountered the Russian Black Sea Fleet 17 nautical miles off Crimea. In a ten-minute firefight at 5–7,000m *Goeben* fired 19 28cm projectiles and struck the flagship *Evstafi* four times, killing 33 men and wounding 35. *Goeben* was hit once in the port III casemate where three 15cm shells detonated and 16 cartridges burned. Thirteen were killed and three were wounded.

On 5–6 December *Goeben* and *Breslau* covered troop transports and on 10 December *Goeben* bombarded Batum. On returning from another covering operation on 26 December *Goeben* was mined off the Bosphorus. The first mine detonated to starboard beneath the conning tower and rent a 50-square-metre hole. However, the torpedo bulkhead held. Two minutes later a second mine detonated just forward of the port wing barbette, renting a 64-square-metre hole. Here the torpedo bulkhead bowed 30cm, but held and a total of 600 tonnes of water entered the ship. Two large 360-tonne caissons had to be constructed to effect rudimentary concrete repairs.

Goeben was combat-ready on 1 May 1915 and a sortie to the Russian coast followed from 6 May to 9 May. A further encounter with the Russian fleet followed on 10 May. *Goeben* opened fire at 16,000m range and the five pre-dreadnought battleships replied with very accurate fire. *Goeben* was hit in the forecastle and on the armoured belt below the waterline, beneath the port II casemate.

A shortage of coal now precluded operations for *Goeben* and it was not until 9–11 August and 5–6 September that she sortied again. A further operation on 8 January 1916 saw *Goeben* encounter the Russian dread-nought *Imperatritsa Ekaterina*. *Goeben* fired five salvos at maximum range but they fell short. However, the Russian fire continued for 30 minutes and the last of the 150 12in shells fired was ranged at 22,500m. *Goeben* escaped with only splinter damage.

On 4–6 February *Goeben* covered a troop transfer and on 4 July 1916 bombarded Tuapse. In summer 1917 *Goeben* was refitted and on 4 September Vizeadmiral von Rebeur-Pachwitz replaced Vizeadmiral Souchon. On 16 December an armistice was signed with Russia and hostilities in the Black Sea ceased.

The next operation took place on 20 January 1918 when *Goeben* and *Breslau* raided the British at Imbros. At 0610hrs a mine struck *Goeben* in compartments X and XI, but the vessel continued the operation. At Imbros the British monitors *Ragan* and *M28* were sunk by the German cruisers at a range of 9,300m. Further vessels and shore targets were taken under fire. While continuing the operation, *Breslau* struck five mines and sank and *Goeben* was forced to retire. However, at 0855hrs she struck a mine to port, forward of the wing barbette. At 0948hrs a third mine was struck on the starboard side in compartments III and IV, but likewise the effect was small. *Goeben* was then attacked by about ten enemy aircraft and owing to confusion she ran aground on Nagara Bank at 1132hrs and was unable to get free. She remained stranded until 26 January when *Torgut Reis* towed *Goeben* off and took her to Constantinople.

Goeben docked in Sevastopol in June, but only the forward mine hit was repaired in Constantinople from 7 August to 19 October, the others waiting until after the war. On 2 November *Goeben* was formally handed over to Turkey as *Yavuz Sultan Selim*. She survived as a museum ship until 1973 when she was scrapped.

CRUISER *J* – *SEYDLITZ*

At the beginning of 1909, further definition was required regarding the development of the German *Großen Kreuzer* type. The General Navy Department requested the State Secretary to define the improvements required for the cruiser of 1910, the new-building *J*. Korvettenkapitän Vollerthun was given the responsibility of putting the basis for future development on paper. He stated that since *Invincible*, the *Großen Kreuzer* were more and more expected to have the qualities of a fast battleship, and that it was the aim to make as many of the legally authorized dreadnoughts as possible capable of combat in the battle line. It was a clear statement of intention. With this Korvettenkapitän Vollerthun recognized the difference between copying the British battlecruisers, with their limited ability for a fleet battle, and developing the German type. He endorsed the German evolution for 'employment against battleships', to which Tirpitz reacted with an emotional 'No! Against cruisers!' Nevertheless, Vollerthun's final comment was emphatic: 'British Battleship-cruisers, our *Kreuzer-battleships*.' He had summed up an arms race in four words.

In spite of these arguments financial constraints meant that practically the *Kreuzer* size could not be increased above that of the battleships, and therefore there was again a trade off between speed and battle capabilities on a limited displacement, at least on paper. A memorandum from the General Navy Department set out some guidelines: speed as for *G*; either 8 x 30.5cm or 10 x 28cm guns; no weakening of offensive power. Triple turrets were considered, however, the 28cm cannon seemed acceptable, at least for 1910.

Seydlitz at a naval review before the war, manning her side. The very light grey colour used on German ships is plainly evident. (Courtesy of Stuart Haller)

In August 1909 the Reichstag reiterated there be no cost increases, and a third sister to *G* was therefore considered, but rejected. Meanwhile, Tirpitz was applying commercial pressure to reduce costs and pressured Blohm & Voss for a discount. He did negotiate some reductions, including successful discounts with armour manufacturers Krupp and Dillingen.

On 27 January 1910 the Kaiser approved the design for *Seydlitz*, at a slight cost increase over *Moltke*.

SEYDLITZ – SPECIFICATIONS

Building dockyard:		Blohm & Voss
Contract:		21 March 1910
Building number:		209
Keel laying:		4 February 1910
Launch:		30 March 1912
Commissioned:		22 May 1913
Displacement:	Designed:	24,988 tonnes
	Loaded:	28,550 tonnes
Length:		200m
Beam:		28.5m
Draught:	Construction:	9.09m
	Loaded:	9.29m
Moulded depth:		13.88m
Performance:	Designed:	63,000shp
	Maximum:	89,738shp
Revolutions per minute:	Designed:	-
	Maximum:	329
Speed:	Designed:	26.5 knots
	Maximum attained:	28.1 knots
Fuel:	Construction:	1,000 tonnes
	Maximum:	3,600 tonnes
Range:		4,200 nautical miles at 14 knots
Cost:		44.685 million marks
Compartments:		17
Double bottom (as % of length):		76
Crew:		43 officers
		1,025 men

Armament

Seydlitz was armed with 10 x 28cm SK L/50 cannon of the same model as in *Moltke*. They were mounted in Drh.L C/1910 mountings, but the elevation and range were the same as *Moltke*, and the same improvements were made in 1916. The ammunition was identical, although 87 shells per gun were carried.

The medium calibre artillery was the same with 12 x 15cm pieces. Initially 12 x 8.8cm SK L/45 guns were fitted, but as with previous classes they were removed and their apertures were welded closed. In 1915 two 8.8cm Flak were fitted to the aft superstructure. The torpedo outfit was the same as in *Moltke*.

Armour

With *Seydlitz* the armour thickness was once again increased. The main belt was 100mm aft, 300mm in the citadel and 100mm forward. Casemate armour was 150mm with 35mm roofs. The forward conning tower was 350mm and the aft conning tower was 200mm thick. Turrets had 250mm vertical armour, and the roofs were 100/70mm thick. Deck armour varied from 80mm aft to 30mm, with 50mm sloping armour. The torpedo bulkhead was 50mm in front of the barbettes, and 30mm otherwise. The barbette armour was 230mm. However, as with all British and German ships of the period, this thickness was reduced where the barbette was shielded by the belt armour. The armour was Krupp cemented and nickel steel.

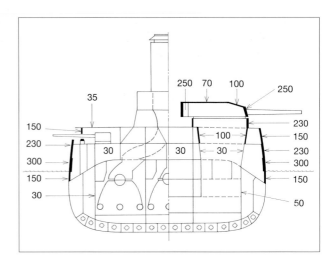

Sea keeping

The *Seydlitz* was a good sea ship, with gentle movements. Like *Moltke*, however, she manoeuvred ponderously and while turning well was also heavy. The metacentric height was 3.12m. Speed loss with helm was as *Moltke*.

Disposition of armour (given in mm) for *Seydlitz*.

Machinery

In Seydlitz the number of boilers was increased to 27 navy type Schulz Thorneycroft, giving steam at a pressure of 235psi or 16 atmospheres. There were five boiler rooms. From 1916 tar-oil supplemental burners were fitted in time for service at the Skagerrak Battle.

There were two sets of Parsons turbines. The forward and aft engine rooms were each partitioned into three, with the high-pressure turbines on the outer shafts in the forward wing rooms, and the low-pressure turbines on the inner shafts in the larger aft engine room. The centre compartment of the forward engine room was used for auxiliary machinery. The shafts drove four propellers of 3.88m diameter. The two rudders were fitted in tandem. Six turbo dynamos provided 1800kw of power at 220 volts.

General characteristics and changes

Seydlitz was easily recognizable by her higher forecastle. Spotting tops were fitted in 1914 and the torpedo nets were discarded in late 1916. From 1917 square rafts were carried on the turret walls. Late in the war a light derrick was fitted to the aft superstructure. Large concrete patches were later conspicuous, covering shellfire damage on B turret and C barbette.

Namesake

Seydlitz was named after Friedrich Wilhelm Freiherr von Seydlitz-Kurzbach (3 February 1721–27 August 1773), General der Kavallerie of Frederick the Great.

Service record

Commanders:

Kapitän zur See Moritz von Egidy	May 1913–October 1917
Kapitän zur See Wilhelm Tägert	October 1917
Kapitän zur See Moritz von Egidy	November 1917
Kapitän zur See Wilhelm Tägert	November 1917–December 1918
Kapitänleutnant Brauer	Internment

Seydlitz was a further development of the *Moltke* at around 14m longer, but 1m narrower. She was launched by General der Kavallerie von Kleist on 30 March 1912. On 22 May 1913 she was commissioned with the crew from *Yorck* and following trials she joined the assembled High Sea Fleet near

Helgoland and went on manoeuvres. On 23 June 1914 the BdA, Commander of Reconnaissance Forces, Kontreadmiral Hipper, transferred his flag from *Moltke* to *Seydlitz*, a position which it held, with brief interruptions, until 26 October 1917. *Seydlitz* went on the interrupted cruise to Norway in July 1914.

Seydlitz led the Reconnaissance Forces in the coastal raid on Great Yarmouth on 2–4 November. On 20 November an advance was made north of Helgoland to integrate *Derfflinger* into I AG. On 15–16 December *Seydlitz* led the attack on Hartlepool. There was battle contact with four destroyers and *Seydlitz* was hit three times by coastal artillery. On the return journey I AG was not supported by the High Sea Fleet and an opportunity was missed to join battle with an inferior part of the Grand Fleet.

The next operation took place on 23–24 January and resulted in the battle at Dogger Bank. During the battle *Seydlitz* expended around 390 28cm projectiles and made many of the 24 hits made on the British ships. In return she was struck by just three shells. The first hit at 1025hrs struck the forecastle and did little damage. The last at 1125hrs struck the armoured belt amidships and likewise caused little damage. It was the second hit by a 13.5in at 1043hrs that caused severe damage. The shell struck the upper deck aft and then hit the barbette of D turret. The 230mm thick armour was holed but the shell was kept out. However, a broken piece of armour and flash flame entered the barbette and ignited the fore and main charges found there. The flames went upwards to the turret and down to the magazine and ignited charges found there. The crew of the working chamber tried to escape to C turret and in so doing

ABOVE **Although this photograph is of the battleship *Kronprinz*, it shows to good effect the protection afforded by the torpedo bulkhead system. On 4 November 1916 *Kronprinz* was torpedoed by the submarine *J1*. The photograph shows the inner compartment, the so-called protective bunker. To the left it can be seen that the gangway longitudinal bulkhead has been ruptured. However, the effect on the armoured torpedo bulkhead to the right is negligible. Some coal can be seen behind the dockyard worker on the ladder.**

RIGHT **A view of *Seydlitz*' conning tower and A turret. This picture offers a good view of the various periscopes on the tower and the rangefinder fitted to the Artillery Direction Position, the raised part of the heavily armoured conning tower. On top of A turret are vents for expelling gases, and at the rear the hatches for installing sub calibre guns. Each turret also has a rangefinder fitted at the front, in this case just behind the life rafts. (Courtesy of Stuart Haller)**

allowed the flash flames to enter there, and again the propellant charges were ignited. The flames that engulfed these two turrets flared mast high and caused the deaths of 165 men. Only the resolute action by Pumpenmeister Wilhelm Heidkamp in flooding the magazines of C and D turrets averted disaster. *Seydlitz* was repaired in the Imperial Dockyard, Wilhelmshaven from 25 January to 31 March 1915.

On 17–18 April, 21–22 April, 17–18 May and 29–30 May 1915, *Seydlitz* took part in fleet operations. From 3 to 21 August I AG, with *Seydlitz*, *Moltke* and *von der Tann*, took part in the Riga Gulf operation, forming a covering group. On 11–12 September I AG covered a mining operation by II AG to Terschelling Bank. On 23–24 October a further fleet advance followed. On 24 November *Seydlitz* was briefly aground in the Kaiser Wilhelm canal. On 4 December, while exiting the Kiel Canal, *Seydlitz* ran over a net barrier and divers found her tangled in her starboard screws.

A copy of a postcard of *Seydlitz* in the large floating dock at the Imperial Dockyard, Kiel before the war. Germany relied heavily on floating docks and in addition to the Imperial yards the private dockyards also maintained them.

On 3–4 March 1916 the I AG participated in the first operation by the new Fleet Chief, Vizeadmiral Scheer – the reception of the auxiliary cruiser *Möwe*. A fleet advance into the Hoofden followed from 5 to 7 March.

On 24 March 1916 *Seydlitz* set out on an operation to bombard Lowestoft, this time under Kontreadmiral Boedicker. (Vizeadmiral Hipper had sciatica and was on leave.) At 1548hrs *Seydlitz* received a mine hit, near the starboard broadside torpedo room. Just as with *Moltke*, although some torpedo heads were rent open they failed to detonate. A hole 90 square metres in size was rent in the side of the ship and a total of 1,400 tonnes of water flooded into the ship. Twelve men perished. Despite the hit being outside the area protected by the torpedo bulkhead, the flooding could be controlled and *Seydlitz* was able to return to Wilhelmshaven under her own power at 15 knots. Repairs were completed on 22 May but a flooding test of the torpedo room on 23–24 May revealed more work was required, so that *Seydlitz* was finally ready for service on 29 May.

A planned fleet advance had been postponed while waiting for *Seydlitz* and the battlecruiser went into the Skagerrak Battle as tactical number 3. Highlights of this battle for *Seydlitz* were:

1650hrs	Opens fire on *Queen Mary*.
1655hrs	Heavy hit in compartment XIII. Starboard forward switch room fails.
1657hrs	Heavy hit on working chamber of C turret. Turret fails, but a repetition of the devastation incurred at Dogger Bank was avoided by new precautions.
1736hrs	Fire from *Seydlitz* and *Derfflinger* destroys *Queen Mary*.
1757hrs	Torpedo hit in forecastle.
1810hrs	B turret hit.
1903hrs	Water penetrating compartments XIV, XV and XVI.
2027hrs	Right gun of E turret put out of action.
2130hrs	Hit on D turret and bridge.

A: SMS *von der Tann*

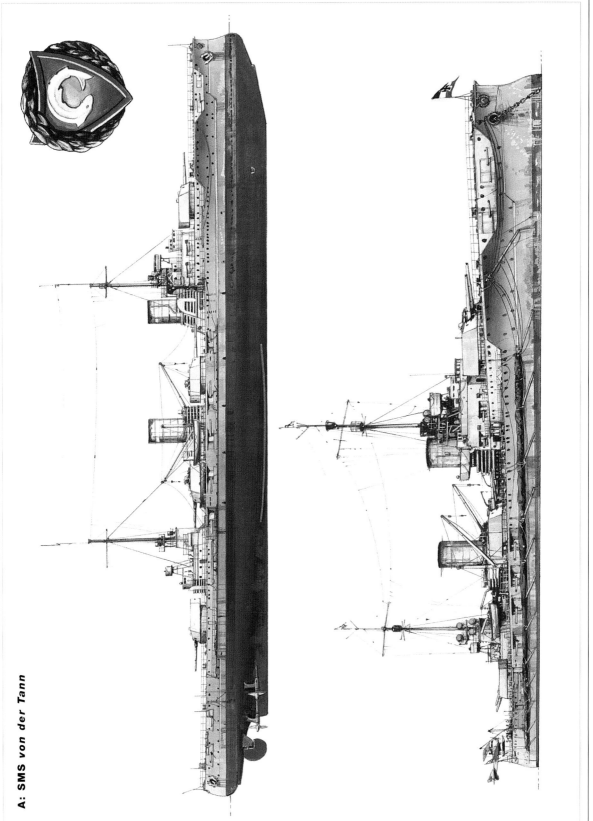

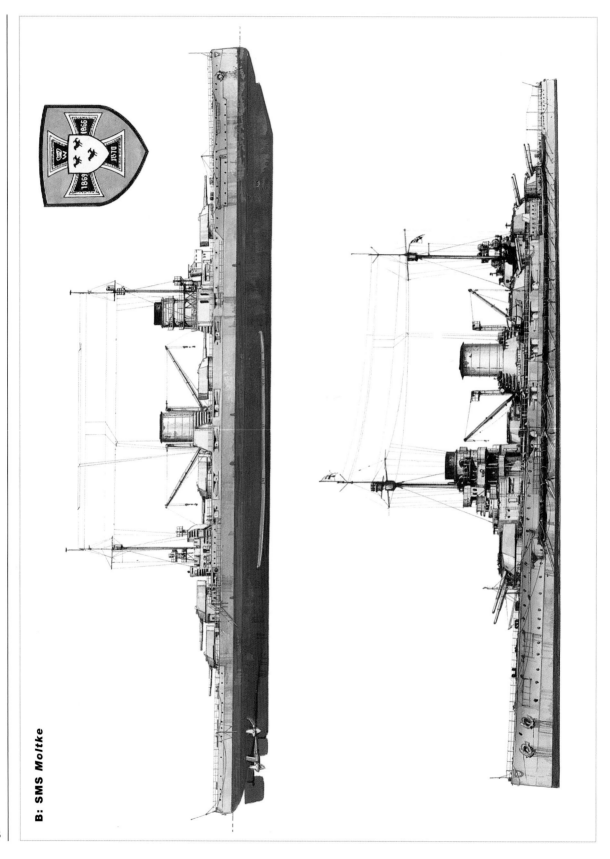

B: SMS *Moltke*

C: Seydlitz at Dogger Bank

D: SMS LÜTZOW

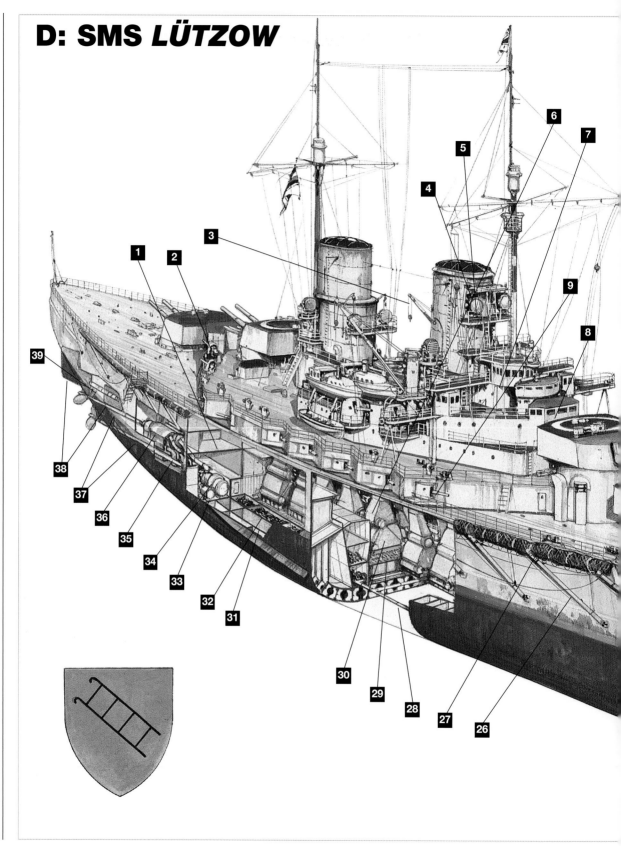

KEY

1 12in shell room
2 3.5in (88mm) guns
3 Boat crane
4 Smoke cover for forward searchlight platform
5 Searchlights
6 Boiler uptakes
7 Signal and admiral's bridge
8 Command bridge
9 5.9in (150mm) guns
10 8 12in (305mm) guns
11 Capstans
12 Capstan room
13 Galley
14 Stores
15 Crew
16 Galley provisions
17 Lower platform deck
18 Forward torpedo tube
19 Torpedo room
20 Trim cell

21 Torpedo store
22 Side torpedo tube
23 Armoured deck
24 Lower between deck
25 Upper between deck
26 Anti-torpedo booms
27 Anti-torpedo netting
28 Main drainage pipe
29 88mm munitions
30 Boilers
31 Protective bunkers
32 Coal bunkers
33 Auxiliary condenser
34 High-pressure turbine
35 Cool water pumps
36 Main condenser
37 Propeller shafts
38 Twin rudder
39 Stern torpedo tube

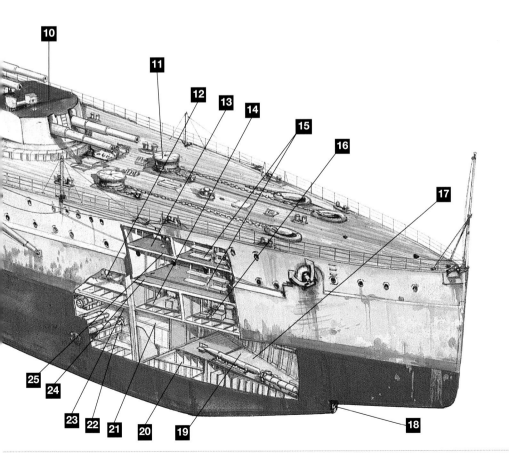

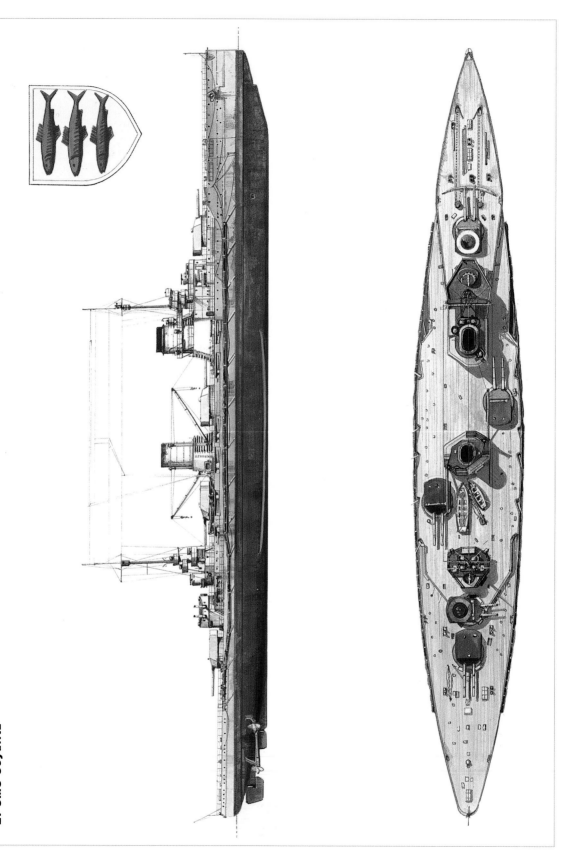

E: SMS _Seydlitz_

F: *Lützow* in the Skagerrak Battle

F

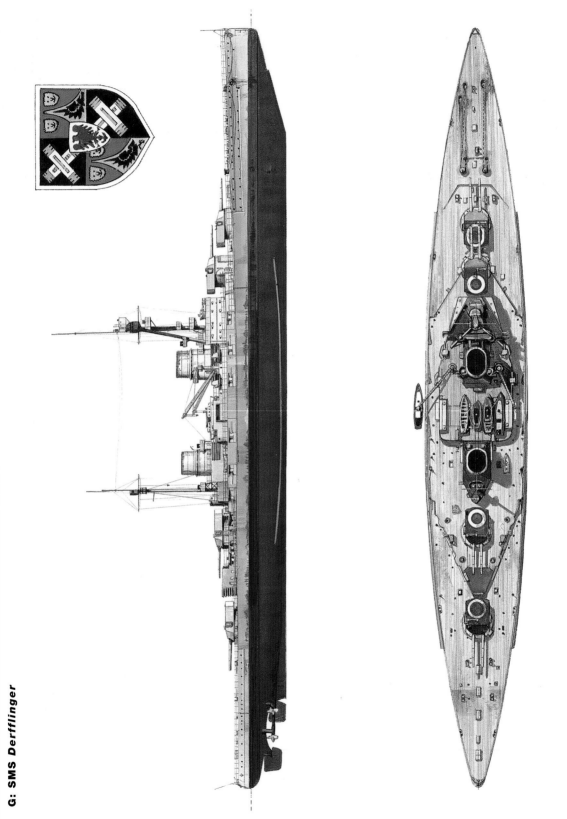

G: *SMS Derfflinger*

Seydlitz returning from the Skagerrak Battle. This was her most critical phase of damage, well down by the bow and before the assistance of pump steamers arrived. It was estimated that a total of 5,308 tonnes of water had flooded the ship.

Seydlitz had been hit 25 times by shells and by one torpedo and in return fired 376 heavy projectiles and made around ten hits, the last four coming from 76 shots. During a night encounter with three British battleships she escaped by flashing their own recognition signal and turning away under cover of smoke. At around 0340hrs on 1 June she found Horns Reef, when the deep lying forecastle scraped over it. Because both *Seydlitz'* gyro-compasses had failed the small cruiser *Pillau* was dispatched to pilot her home. By around 1530hrs the situation became critical for the *Große Kreuzer*. She was badly down by the bow and the wind had reached strength 8. Only the buoyant broadside torpedo room was keeping *Seydlitz* afloat and preparations were made to evacuate the wounded. However, soon two pump steamers arrived and with the help of dockyard tugs the heavily damaged ship was brought safely home. On the morning of 2 June the outer Jade River was reached, and the following day *Seydlitz* entered Entrance III of Wilhelmshaven Dock. At worst there had been 5,308 tonnes of water in the ship.

Seydlitz was repaired in the Imperial Dockyard, Wilhelmshaven from 15 June to 1 October 1916 and after individual training was again combat-ready in November. Although she again served as flagship for Vizeadmiral Hipper until 26 October 1917, an office administration ship, *Niobe*, was placed at his disposal on 20 August 1916.

On 4–5 November *Seydlitz* went to Bovbjerg on the Danish coast, together with *Moltke*, the 2nd Division of I Squadron, III Squadron including *Bayern* and IV AG to recover the stranded *U-Bootes U20* and *U30*.

Throughout the remainder of the war, the German High Sea forces were continually occupied covering minesweeping operations, as precedence was given to the *U-Boote* campaign.

On 23 April 1918 *Seydlitz* participated in the last advance by the High Sea Fleet to Norway. Between 30 July and 1 August 1918 she also participated in the operation to sweep 'Route 500', during which the minesweeper *M6* was lost. At the end of October *Seydlitz* stood ready for the planned operation by the fleet. *Seydlitz* was part of the fleet interned at Scapa Flow and was scuttled on 21 June 1919. She was raised in November 1928 and scrapped.

Seydlitz was one of the most popular and famous ships of the Imperial Navy, and was always know as a 'happy ship'. Her motto was 'Allen Voran' – 'All ahead'.

CRUISERS OF THE *DERFFLINGER* CLASS

The new *Panzerkreuzer*
Derfflinger re-entering the
dockyard of Blohm & Voss,
Hamburg in September 1914.
(Courtesy of Carsten Steinhorst)

Quite correctly the ships of the *Derfflinger* class were considered to be the best battlecruisers completed up until the end of World War I. Aesthetically they were also the most handsome. Design work was begun in October 1910 and continued until October 1912 and the class consisted of the sisterships *Derfflinger* and *Lützow* and the near-sister *Hindenburg*. The design represented the change to a new generation of German *Großen Kreuzer*.

After the final design of cruiser *J* there were still outstanding issues for the following design. In April 1910 the General Navy Department was asked to prepare the requirements for the cruiser of 1911. The issues were primarily the number of shafts and the types of machinery and armament. A three-shaft arrangement would allow the employment of a diesel engine on the centre shaft. The advantages of this system were better thermal efficiency, easier transfer of fuel, saving in personnel and the price. The General Department thought the change to 30.5cm calibre guns was essential. The weight increase of 8 x 30.5cm guns over 10 x 28cm guns was just 36 tonnes and was warranted by the fact that the latest British battleships were fitted with 300mm armour. If the battlecruisers were expected to fight in the line the increase was mandatory. However, Tirpitz disagreed and the matter remained unresolved. Meanwhile Geheim Oberbaurät Veith determined that the large diesels were still not ready.

On 1 September a decision was taken for 8 x 30.5cm cannon on the centreline. The armoured protection was to remain as with *Seydlitz*. In the interim the Kaiser had become concerned about the British 'we want eight' ship programme, which was instigated by the public and media who, spurred on by rumours of German secret shipbuilding, coined the phrase 'we want eight and we won't wait', pressurizing the government to approve eight ships in 1909. So the Kaiser, in turn, desired the cruisers' building time reduced from three years to 24 months. This reduction was not feasible, as the armour producers could not keep up production and neither could the armament manufacturer. The time revision would also entail a change in the payment plan, as the four-yearly instalments would be reduced to three. The Reichstag would have to agree to this.

To save weight a new type of construction technique was used that had hitherto been used on the small cruisers. The longitudinal frame system was used for construction of the lower ship's bottom. Previous large warships had been constructed with a system of mixed longitudinal and transverse frames. With an increase in the ship's length the demands on the longitudinal strength increased, and these demands could be met, with a lower weight, by employing a pure longitudinal frame method of construction.

The hull was to be partitioned in two, as with *von der Tann*, and this allowed coal to be stored inside the torpedo bulkhead. On 8 June 1910, oil boilers were mentioned for the first time. The advantages of oil were less weight, smaller boilers for the same performance, and saving in serving personnel. Steam could be raised rapidly and there was no tell-tale smoke plume. The only major drawback was that the navy would have to rely on foreign producers. Therefore eight of the 22 coal boilers were replaced with four pure oil-fired boilers. Provision was made for the later fitment of Frahm anti-roll tanks. Nevertheless the trial cruise of *von der Tann* had revealed that the tanks only reduced the roll by 33 per cent.

The cruiser *Ersatz Kaiserin Augusta*, later *Lützow*, was to be a repeat building. For the first time since *Blücher*, the contract went to a company other than Blohm & Voss. The reasons given were a desire to break the monopoly of Blohm & Voss and also for geographic advantages. The third ship, *Ersatz Hertha*, later *Hindenburg*, was slightly larger and was built at the Imperial Dockyard, Wilhelmshaven.

DERFFLINGER CLASS – SPECIFICATIONS

		Derfflinger	*Lützow*	*Hindenburg*
Building yard:		Blohm & Voss, Hamburg	Schichau, Danzig	Imperial Dockyard, Wilhelmshaven
Contract:		1912	1912	20 April 1913
Building number:		213	885	34
Keel laid:		30 March 1912	15 May 1912	1 October 1913
Launched:		12 July 1913	29 November 1913	1 August 1915
Commissioned:		1 September 1914	8 August 1915	10 May 1917
Displacement:	Designed:	26,600 tonnes	26,741 tonnes	26,947 tonnes
	Loaded:	31,200 tonnes	—	31,500 tonnes
Length:		210m	210m	212.4m
Beam:		29m	29m	29m
Draught:		9.2m	9.2m	9.29m
Moulded depth:		14.75m	14.75m	—
Performance:	Designed:	63,000shp	—	72,000shp
	Overload:	76,624shp	80,988shp	95,777shp
Revolutions:		280	277	290
Speed:	Designed:	25.5 knots	—	26.6 knots
	Maximum:	26.5 knots[1]	26.4 knots[2]	27 knots
Fuel:	Normal:	750 tonnes coal	750 tonnes coal	750 tonnes coal
(tonnes)		250 tonnes oil	250 tonnes oil	250 tonnes oil
	Maximum:	3,500 tonnes coal	3,700 tonnes coal	3,700 tonnes coal
		1,000 tonnes oil	1,000 tonnes oil	1,200 tonnes oil
Range:		5,600nm at 14 knots	5,600nm at 14 knots	6,100nm at 14 knots
Cost:		56 million marks	58 million marks	59 million marks
Compartments:		16	17	17
Double bottom:		65%	65%	65%
Crew:		44 officers 1,068 men	Admiral Staff 14 officers 62 men	Same

1. These speeds were run in shallow water because of the war, and in deeper water speeds 2 knots higher could have been expected.
2. On 19 May 1916 *Lützow* achieved a speed of 27.9 knots, again in shallow water.

Armament

The main armament of this class was 8 x 30.5cm L/50 SK cannon. This gun could fire with a rate of three projectiles per minute, and the 405.5kg shell was propelled at a muzzle velocity of 900mps. The guns were fitted in the Drh.L C/1912 mounts on *Derfflinger* and *Lützow*, and the Drh.L C/1913 mounts on *Hindenburg*. Each turret was electrically trained and the guns were hydraulically elevated to a maximum of 13.5° before 1916, which gave a range of 18,000m, and after 1916 this was improved to 16.5° and 20,400m. As on the other cruisers, the fore charge came in a silk bag, and the main charge was enclosed in a brass cartridge. A total of 720 30.5cm shells were carried for a total of 90 per gun, 65 AP and 25 semi-AP. With A, B and C turrets, the magazines were below the shell rooms, on the lower platform deck, whilst with D turret this was reversed. *Lützow* was completed with gyroscopic firing gear (AG) but it was not used in combat. Subsequently *Derfflinger* and *Hindenburg* were also fitted with this equipment.

The medium-calibre armament was the 15cm SK L/45 cannon, in a MPL C/06.11 mount, and a MPL C/13 mount on *Hindenburg*. *Derfflinger* carried 12 of these cannon as one per side was deleted to make space for the Frahm tanks. *Lützow* and *Hindenburg* each carried 14 x 15cm pieces. A shell outfit of 160 rounds per gun was carried. The guns initially could be ranged to 13,500m, and later out to 16,800m.

As built *Derfflinger* carried 8 x 8.8cm SK L/45 cannon, four in the forward superstructure and four mounted around C turret. Four 8.8cm Flak L/45 were mounted about the forward funnel. By 1916 the four guns in the forward superstructure had been removed. After her completion *Lützow* was fitted with 4 x 8.8cm Flak around the aft funnel, whilst *Hindenburg* carried the four Flak grouped around the forward funnel. *Derfflinger* had four 50cm torpedo tubes while the other two ships carried 60cm H8 torpedoes, and the outfit was increased to 12 torpedoes. These torpedoes had an increased warhead weight of 210kg and could range to 6,000m at 36 knots, or 14,000m at 30 knots.

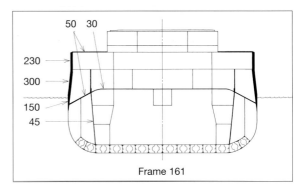

Cross section of *Derfflinger*'s armour (given in mm).

Derfflinger in Schillig Roads early in the war. (Courtesy of Carsten Steinhorst)

Trials with seaplanes took place aboard *Derfflinger* in early August 1915. A derrick was fitted amidships and is shown here hoisting Brandenburg W aircraft No.234 aboard. (Courtesy of Carsten Steinhorst)

Armour

The armour of the *Derfflinger* class was similar in thickness to that of *Seydlitz*. The main belt was 100mm aft, 300mm in the citadel and 120mm forward. The casemate armour was 230mm with 50mm roofs. The forward conning tower was 350mm and the aft conning tower was 200mm thick. The turrets had 270mm faces, 225mm walls, and the roofs were 110/80mm. The barbettes were 260mm. The deck armour varied from 80mm aft to 30mm, with 50mm sloping armour. The torpedo bulkhead was 45mm thick. The armour was Krupp cemented and nickel steel.

Sea keeping

The ships of the *Derfflinger* class were excellent sea ships with pleasant motion. They manoeuvred well, but slowly – they turned well but were slow to answer the helm. The metacentric height was 2.6m, which was reduced from the previous class to reduce 'stiffness'. With hard-over rudder there was a 65 per cent speed loss and 11° heel. In a swell the casemates were reported as wet.

Machinery

The six boiler rooms were divided down the centre by a longitudinal bulkhead. There were 14 double coal Schulz naval boilers working at 235psi. They were provided with supplemental tar-oil firing from 1916. The four double oil-fired boilers occupied the forward two boiler rooms.

There were two sets of naval turbines. The forward engine rooms were adjacent to C turret and housed the high-pressure turbines, working on the outer shafts. The turbo generators were installed on the deck above them. The aft engine rooms were between C and D turrets, giving the characteristic gap between these turrets. They contained the low-pressure turbines, which worked the inner shafts, and condensers. The shafts drove four propellers of 3.9m in diameter, whilst *Hindenburg* had 4m diameter propellers. The two rudders were fitted in tandem.

The two turbo dynamos and two diesel dynamos provided 220 volts at 1,160kw in *Derfflinger*, 1,520kw in *Lützow* and 2,120kw in *Hindenburg*. The diesel dynamos were located below the forward magazines, in the *Stauung*, or hold.

Derfflinger's machinery weighed a total of 3,269 tonnes, whereas that of *Princess Royal* weighed 5,019 tonnes. A further comparison of weights as a percentage of total displacement is as follows:

	LION	QUEEN MARY	TIGER	LÜTZOW
Armament	12.3	12.5	12.65	12.7
Machinery	20.2	20.2	20.7	14.2
Armour	24.2	24.5	25.9	35.5
Hull	36.5	36.1	34.3	30.5

General characteristics and changes

The ships of this class were easily distinguishable from one another. *Derfflinger*'s funnels were of uneven height and had deep caps. *Lützow* was built with even height funnels with deep caps, but after she was transferred to Imperial Dockyard, Kiel for completion, the forward funnel was fully jacketed. *Hindenburg* had both with smaller caps. *Derfflinger* and *Lützow* were completed with pole masts. However, the latter's commander requested a tripod mast be built in whilst fitting out. This remained undone, but during repairs after the Skagerrak Battle *Derfflinger* had a wide-spread tripod mast fitted. *Hindenburg* was completed with a narrower based tripod mast.

Trials carrying seaplanes were carried out on *Derfflinger* in August 1915.

Namesake – *Derfflinger*

Derfflinger was named after Georg Reichsfreiherr von Derfflinger, born on 10 March 1606 and died on 4 February 1695. He was a Generalfeldmarschall and leader of the Brandenburg cavalry.

Service record – *Derfflinger*

Commanders:

Kapitän zur See von Reuter	September 1914–September 1915
Kapitän zur See Heinrich	September 1915–April 1916
Kapitän zur See Johannes Hartog	April 1916–December 1917
Fregattenkapitän/	
Kapitän zur See von Schlick	December 1917–November 1918
Kapitän zur See Walter Hildebrand	November 1918–December 1918
Korvettenkapitän Pastuszyk	Internment

Most of the casualties aboard *Derfflinger* occurred when C and D turrets were hit. A 15in shell struck the roof of D turret and detonated inside, burning the cartridges there and killing 75 of the turret crew. A further 15in shell from *Revenge* struck C barbette, and penetrated and destroyed this turret. Only one man was saved from D turret, and six from C turret. The entrance holes of these shells can be seen. It can also be seen that the spent cartridge cases of the main charges have been collected and stacked adjacent to the barbettes.

A fine view of *Derfflinger* at anchor in Wilhelmshaven in 1915. (Courtesy of Stuart Haller)

The new-building *K* was ready for launching on 14 June 1913 and was christened *Derfflinger* by the wife of General der Kavallerie August von Mackensen. However, after the hull had moved just 30–40cm she stuck fast and only on 12 July was the ship successfully launched. One of the wooden sledges had overheated and jammed.

In spring 1914 a dockyard crew took *Derfflinger* around the Skagen to Kiel. The vessel was allocated to I AG at the end of October, but because of turbine damage could not join this unit until 16 November. A short advance followed on 20 November. On 15–16 December *Derfflinger* participated in the bombardment of Scarborough and Whitby.

During the Dogger Bank Battle *Derfflinger* inflicted much damage to *Lion* while suffering only one hit herself – a 13.5in burst on the 300mm belt. Near misses caused some leakage and *Derfflinger* was again combat-ready on 14 February. *Derfflinger* took part in the fleet advances of March, April and May, but on 28 June she suffered damage to the starboard low-pressure turbine and was in dock until August. On 31 August *Derfflinger* returned to the North Sea and on 11–12 September covered the minelaying operation to Swarte Bank. A fleet advance followed on 23–24 October.

The year 1916 saw increased activity by the High Sea Fleet and under the new Fleet Chief, Vizeadmiral Scheer, an advance in the Hoofden was made on 6–7 March, and on 25 March a counter-thrust was carried out against British light forces. On 24–25 April a coastal bombardment of Lowestoft was conducted and a running battle with British light forces followed.

During the Skagerrak Battle *Derfflinger* was tactical number 2 and was struck by shells 21 times. Highlights of *Derfflinger*'s battle were:

1726hrs	Under the fire of *Derfflinger* and *Seydlitz*, the *Queen Mary* explodes.
1819hrs	First hit strikes the bows.
1930hrs	*Derfflinger* firing on *Invincible* when the British ship blows up.
2014–2020hrs	*Derfflinger* in a hail of fire and hit nine times.
2014hrs	D turret hit and put out of action.
2016hrs	C turret barbette hit and turret put out of action.

Derfflinger was also hit by two 6in shells and seven 4in shells. She suffered 157 dead and 26 wounded, the highest figures for a ship not sunk. *Derfflinger* returned to harbour with over 3,000 tonnes of water in the ship. The success of this cruiser during the battle led to the British sailors giving her the nickname 'Iron Dog'.

Provisional repairs were carried out at Wilhelmshaven and then *Derfflinger* transferred to Howaldts dockyard in Kiel where she was under repair until 15 October, a period which included the installation of her

A particularly fine view of *Derfflinger* after the war shows how wide the legs of the tripod mast were spread. A very tall mast was initially fitted, but this was shortened later.

tripod mast. After individual training in the Baltic *Derfflinger* was combat-ready in November.

Throughout the remainder of the war the large ships were active covering smaller units in minesweeping and escorting *U-Boote* convoys. At the beginning of November *Derfflinger* covered a minelaying operation to Horns Reef and on 17 November put to sea in support of the embattled II AG. In 1918 on 20 April she covered a minelaying operation to Terschelling Bank and on 23–24 April took part in the advance to Norway. On 16 May *Derfflinger* was rammed by the *Sperrbrecher* ('Barrier Breaker', a ship made secure against mines and used to test dangerous waters) *Schwaben* and had to be repaired.

Derfflinger was one of the ships interned at Scapa Flow and was scuttled on 21 June 1919. She was raised in 1939 as the last ship, and breaking up work only began in 1946.

Namesake – *Lützow*

Lützow was named after Ludwig Adolf Freiherr von Lützow (18 May 1782–6 December 1834), the Prussian Generalmajor during the Napoleonic Wars.

Service record – *Lützow*

Commander: Kapitän zur See Harder   8 August 1915–1 June 1916.

The second ship of the *Derfflinger* class, *Ersatz Kaiserin Augusta*, was built in the Schichau dockyard in Danzig. At noon on 29 November 1913 the new ship was christened *Lützow* by Hofmarschall Maximilian Graf von Pückler, Freiherr von Groditz. *Lützow* was commissioned on 8 August 1915 and then travelled to Kiel on 23 August for final fitting out and arming. Whilst running trials on 25 October *Lützow* suffered serious damage to the port low-pressure turbine and repairs continued in Kiel until the end of January. Further trials followed and were concluded on 19 February 1916. *Lützow* joined I AG on 20 March and returned to the North Sea with it on 24 March.

On 25 March *Lützow* undertook her first operational mission, a counter-thrust against British light forces. A further fleet advance followed on 21–22 April, and the small cruiser *Graudenz* was mined. The coastal bombardment of Yarmouth followed on 23–24 April and *Lützow* served as flagship after *Seydlitz* was mined. She did not fire on the shore but engaged the light cruiser *Conquest* and hit her several times.

A further period of individual training in the Baltic followed. On 16 May *Lützow* arrived for shooting and torpedo practice and on the measured mile on 19 May reached a speed of 27.9 knots. Late on 22 May *Lützow* arrived back off Wilhelmshaven.

On 28 May Vizeadmiral Hipper hoist his flag on *Lützow* and on 30 May the ship passed out of the lock to Schillig Roadstead. The I AG put to sea on 31 May and at 1748hrs that afternoon *Lützow* opened fire in what was not only the largest battleship battle ever – Skagerrak Bank – but was also to be her last battle. The highlights of *Lützow*'s battle were:

1651hrs	First hits on opponent, *Lion*.
1700hrs	First hit on *Lützow*, in the forecastle. Hit on *Lion* destroys Q turret.
1715hrs	Hit wrecks forward dressing station.
1744hrs	*Lützow* hits battleship *Barham*.
1825hrs	Two hits destroy wireless rooms. Vizeadmiral Hipper no longer has wireless contact with Vizeadmiral Scheer.
1916hrs	Opens fire on *Defence*, which explodes after three salvos.
1926–1934hrs	*Lützow* under a hail of fire from III Battlecruiser Squadron. The port broadside and bow torpedo rooms are hit by four 12in shells and the forecastle compartments from XII to XVI immediately fill with water.
1930hrs	The battlecruiser *Invincible* explodes under fire from *Lützow* and *Derfflinger*.
2015hrs	*Lützow* hit five more times. A and B turrets hit.
2215hrs	2,395 tonnes of water in the ship.
0220hrs	Attempt to steer ship stern first fails as the propellers and rudder were coming out of the water and *Lützow* could only steer in a circle. Call to abandon ship.
0247hrs	*Lützow* sinks after being torpedoed by torpedo boat *G38*.

Lützow was the only dreadnought ship to be lost by the Imperial Navy. She was lost because the extensive flooding in the forecastle could not be held as the forward pump group failed, and the centre pump group was unable to cope with the rising water. Shortly before *Lützow* was abandoned it was estimated that there was 8,319 tonnes of water in the ship. The crew

On Thursday, 29 November 1913, at 1200hrs, the new battlecruiser *Lützow* was launched at the Schichau dockyard in Danzig. By coincidence the battleship *Baden* was built on the same slipway, and after *Lützow* was lost the crew were transferred to commission the new battleship – *Baden*.

were saved by four escorting torpedo boats, but the eventual casualty count numbered 128 men.

Namesake – *Hindenburg*

Hindenburg was named after Paul von Beneckendorff und von Hindenburg (2 October 1847–2 August 1934), the Prussian Generalfeldmarschall.

Service record – *Hindenburg*

Commanders:

Kapitän zur See von Karpf	May 1917–November 1917
Korvettenkapitän Oldekop	July 1917
Kapitän zur See Walter Hildebrand	February 1918–November 1918
Korvettenkapitän Heyden	Internment

The third ship of the *Derfflinger* class, *Ersatz Hertha*, was built as an improvement of the original class design. With the outbreak of war the ship was still on the slipway at the Imperial Dockyard, Wilhelmshaven and as this dockyard now became concerned with fitting out the Reserve Fleet ships construction was delayed. Only on 1 August 1915 was she launched as *Hindenburg*. Further construction proceeded slowly due to labour shortages. In April 1917 *Hindenburg* was lightly rammed by the battleship *Helgoland* as she left dock.

On 10 May 1917 *Hindenburg* was commissioned as the last dreadnought to join the Imperial Navy. Trials were completed on 28 October 1917 and *Hindenburg* went from Kiel to Wilhelmshaven on 25 October. On 6 November she undertook picket and security duty with I AG.

On 17 November *Hindenburg* and *Moltke* were operating in support of minesweepers and II AG when they were attacked by strong British forces, including battlecruisers. Nevertheless, the opponents broke off the battle before *Hindenburg* could come into action. On 23 November *Hindenburg* replaced *Seydlitz* as flagship of Vizeadmiral Ritter von Hipper. However, except for operations, the Commander of Reconnaissance Forces used the small cruiser *Niobe* as his office.

On 23–24 April 1918 *Hindenburg* took part in the fleet advance to the latitude of Bergen. The operation was broken off prematurely because of damage to *Moltke* and on 26 April Vizeadmiral Hipper again transferred to *Niobe*. From 27 July to 1 August *Hindenburg* took part, together with I AG in the operation to secure light forces clearing the new route, 'Weg 500'. On 11 August a new Commander of Reconnaissance Forces was appointed as Vizeadmiral Hipper had been promoted to Commander of the High Sea Fleet. On 12 August Kontreadmiral von Reuter hoist his flag on *Hindenburg* which now served continuously as flagship. *Hindenburg* stood ready for the operation on 30 October 1918. When this undertaking was called off *Hindenburg* went into dock on 2 November and was among the ships to be interned at Scapa Flow.

Hindenburg was scuttled on 21 June 1919 and was the only ship to be sunk on an even keel. The ship was raised in 1930 and subsequently scrapped.

A fine view of *Lützow* underway. The speed spheres on the fore mast indicate full speed. (Courtesy of Carsten Steinhorst)

THE LESSONS OF DOGGER BANK

The battle of Dogger Bank took place on 24 January 1915 when the German I and II Reconnaissance Groups advanced to the middle of the North Sea on a mission to interrupt British light forces thought to be operating there. In his diary Kontreadmiral Hipper had warned against such an unsupported undertaking several times, but nevertheless he acted on instructions and began the operation. British Naval Intelligence intercepted and deciphered German wireless signals which enabled the Royal Navy Battlecruiser Fleet to spring a trap on the German forces. In the ensuing battle the Germans lost *Blücher* and over 900 men.

The battle on the Dogger Bank was obviously a British victory and the press rejoiced in it, but it sent all the wrong messages to the victors, whilst the Germans learned valuable lessons.

The loss of *Blücher* and heavy damage to *Seydlitz*, and then the retirement of Kontreadmiral Hipper's forces, masked the other events of the day. At 1043hrs the second hit on *Seydlitz* struck the aft deck and then D turret barbette, breaking off a piece of armour that penetrated the working chamber and ignited the fore and main charges on the loading rails found there. Flash flame shot upwards and downwards through the hoists and set fire to the charges on the turntable and to those in the hoist room. Only those charges with their container lids on failed to ignite. The crew of D turret attempted to escape to C turret and opened the interconnecting bulkhead door. This allowed an instantaneous flash to pass to C cartridge hoist room and the catastrophe was repeated. Although some main charges in their cases were not burnt, in a few seconds over 6,000kg of powder burnt and both C and D turrets blazed. As related earlier, only resolute action in flooding the magazines saved the ship.

The second hit on *Blücher*, at 1130hrs, penetrated the munition transport rail shaft that ran from C and E turret magazines forward to supply B and F turrets with munitions. A total of 35–40 cartridges on the rails were ignited, the flash passed up to B and F turrets and they erupted in a sea of flame, just as on *Seydlitz*. Shell splinters penetrated the main steam pipe of boiler room III, the steam pressure dropped and *Blücher*'s speed fell to 17 knots. From this point *Blücher* was doomed. Therefore, the third and fourth hits landed on the German ships had decided the battle. *Blücher* was then systematically battered as the range fell, but the other German battlecruisers were hit only twice more.

Some of the conclusions stated in the subsequent German report were as follows: the hoists must be equipped with automatically closing doors; the fore charges must be kept in their tins until they reach the gun, as only these had not burnt; the main charges must be kept protected until they are ready to load; the cartridge tins must only be removed when the cartridge is required, and new bayonet clasps must be introduced; the ready charges must be prevented from piling up in the turret; no projectiles had exploded; and no more fore charges should be allowed than main charges (cartridges). Many of these recommendations had been acted upon by the time of the Skagerrak Battle.

By comparison with *Seydlitz* and *Blücher*, *Lion* had been hit 17 times and *Tiger* was hit seven times. The *Lion* was so badly damaged that she had to be towed home by *Indomitable*. There were no lessons taken by the British about the dangers of cordite fires. The British admirals were more concerned with the superior German rate of fire, which Admiral David Beatty considered in a ratio of five to two. Therefore, in the Skagerrak Battle the British battlecruisers had stockpiled cordite charges, all of which were unprotected in silk bags, throughout the magazine hoists and barbettes, in an attempt to improve the supply to the guns. It was the exact opposite of what the Germans had done.

When *Seydlitz'* C barbette was penetrated at Skagerrak Bank two main and two fore charges burnt and the turret fell out, but two other cartridges, still with their covers on, failed to burn. In *Lützow*'s B turret only one fore charge burnt while a main charge did not. Nevertheless, on *Derfflinger* 20 charges burned in D turret while four did not, and in C turret 14 charges burnt and six remained safe. British battlecruisers fared poorly in comparison.

CONCLUSION

The German *Großen Kreuzer* were excellent fighting ships because of their better weight distribution and weight percentages allocated to armour, machinery, hull and armament. They had better propellant and projectiles, which did not explode when subjected to flash. Their design concept had been well devised, thought through and developed by an exceptional design group. The German 'Kreuzer-Battleships' had defeated the British 'Battleship-Cruisers', and had fought and resisted the most modern and heavily armed battleships. The German battlecruiser concept had been completely vindicated, in spite of restrictive financial constraints.

BIBLIOGRAPHY

Campbell, John, *Jutland*, Conway (1986)
Campbell, N. J. M, *Battlecruisers*, Conway (1978)
Greißmer, Alex, *Große Kreuzer der Kaiserlichen Marine 1906–1918*, Bernard & Graefe (1996)
Gröner, Erich, *Die deutschen Kriegsschiffe 1815–1945*, Bernard & Graefe (1982)
Hildebrand, Hans, *Die Deutschen Kriegsschiffe*, Volumes 1–7, Koehlers (1979)
Koop, Gerhard and Klaus-Peter Schmolke, *Die Großen Kreuzer von der Tann bis Hindenburg*, Bernard & Graefe (1998)
Mäkelä, Matti, *Auf der Spuren der Goeben*, Bernard & Graefe (1979)
von Mantey, Eberhard, *Auf See unbesiegt*, Volumes 1 and 2, J. F. Lehmans (1922)
von Mantey, Eberhard, *Der Krieg zur See 1914-1918. Krieg in der Nordsee*, Volumes 1–7, E. S. Mittler & Sohn (1920–64)
Mukhenikov, V. B., *German Battlecruisers*, St Petersburg (1998)
Ruge, Friedrich, *Warship Profile 14, Seydlitz*, Profile (1972)
Strohbusch, E., *Marine-Rundschau 1975/9 von der Tann*, J. F. Lehmans
Strohbusch, E., *Marine-Rundschau 1976/7 Derfflinger*, J. F. Lehmans
Bundesarchiv-Militärarchiv:
RM3-3449 *Lützow* trials report
BA MA 92-2983 *Lützow* War Diary
N162 Nachlaß Vizeadmiral Hipper

COLOUR PLATE COMMENTARY

A: SMS *VON DER TANN*

Von der Tann was the first German battlecruiser and the first large German warship to be built with turbine propulsion. The vessel was considered a very successful design and created a wonderful impression at the Spithead Review in June 1911. Her proving cruise to South America showed a worldwide deployment capability and also the dependability of her machinery. However, the Frahm anti-rolling tanks were not as successful as predicted and only reduced the roll by 33 per cent. Furthermore, the arrangement of accommodating the officers in the forecastle was not to be repeated.

When commissioned *von der Tann* was the fastest capital ship in the world, a fact that belied the theory that speed could only be bought at the expense of protection. Its main armament of 8 x 28cm guns could be equally deployed to port or starboard, giving the ship a broadside of eight cannon over a wide arc, equal to that of the first German dreadnought, which nevertheless mounted 12 pieces.

B: SMS *MOLTKE*

The battlecruisers *Moltke* and *Goeben* were improvements of the first battlecruiser design and mounted a formidable broadside of 10 x 28cm cannon, which had the ballistic qualities of the 30.5cm pieces of foreign navies. The extent and thickness of the armoured protection was also increased and an increase in boiler output meant that the speed was also marginally improved. The underwater protection system of this class was extensively tested during the war. *Moltke* was torpedoed by submarines on two occasions, and *Goeben* was mined on two occasions, striking two mines in the first instance, and three in the last. Even when struck outside the area protected by the torpedo bulkhead, the effect was minimal compared to foreign capital ships. *Moltke* was always considered as a 'lucky' ship. She visited the United States in 1912, while *Goeben* was deployed to the Mediterranean. *Moltke* was scheduled to go to the East Asiatic Squadron, but the need to replace *Goeben* meant this plan was deferred. The deployment of the first three German battlecruisers to overseas stations showed the worldwide deployment capabilities of the type.

C: *SEYDLITZ* AT DOGGER BANK

A view of *Seydlitz* in action during the battle on the Dogger Bank. British wireless intercepts meant that a battlecruiser force was awaiting Kontreadmiral Hipper when he arrived on the Dogger Bank early on the morning of 24 January 1915. A very long-range action developed and, contrary to the expectations of some German planners prior to the war, the action continued at long range. The range of the German weapons was shown to be inadequate and an improvement was not effected until after the Skagerrak Battle. Nevertheless, despite the improved range the battleship *König* still found herself outranged by the Russian pre-dreadnought *Slava* on 17 October 1917.

When the aft C and D turrets were burnt out, *Seydlitz*' I Artillerie Offizier ordered 'rapid fire' from the remaining turrets: fearing his ship was about to explode he wanted to inflict maximum damage before this could happen.

D: SMS *LÜTZOW*

A battlecruiser of the *Derfflinger* class, *Lützow* was divided into 17 watertight compartments. Between the barbettes the hull was divided into two by a longitudinal bulkhead. To save weight and provide increased strength the longitudinal frame system of construction was used for the lower hull, and the situating of the high-pressure turbine rooms adjacent to C turret magazines saved weight by reducing the length by one compartment. Unfortunately, as with all the German *Panzerkreuzer* except *Blücher*, the armoured torpedo bulkhead was terminated at the

A bow aspect of *Hindenburg* taken after the war shows to good effect the thickness and extent of the armoured belt.

ABOVE **A nice view of *von der Tann* at the Spithead Review for the coronation of King George V in June 1911.**

A view of *Seydlitz* taken from *Moltke* in Wilhelmshaven after the Dogger Bank Battle. The occasion is the visit of the Kaiser to confer decorations on those awarded them. It can be seen that *Seydlitz* still flies the flag of Kontreadmiral Hipper and that the cannon have been removed from the burnt-out C and D turrets. The Artillerie Offizier, Korvettenkapitän Foerster, afterwards wrote: 'A couple of days later the Kaiser came aboard and decorated Leutnant zur See Walter with the Iron Cross, and said to him, "Well, it must have been very warm in that turret." And Walter replied, "Aye, Your Majesty, several thousand degrees."(!)' (Courtesy of Stuart Haller)

forward turret barbette, frame 249. When four 12in shells struck *Lützow* below the waterline and armoured belt forward, outside the area protected by the torpedo bulkhead, the effect was to immediately flood the entire bow below the armoured deck. *Lützow*'s I Artillerie Offizier termed this her 'Achilles Heel'.

The forward two boiler rooms contained the large oil boilers, and the remaining 14 coal boilers were housed aft of these. The high-pressure turbines had the turbo generators mounted on a deck above them, while the low-pressure turbine room contained the main condensers as well. The slender lines aft meant that the rudders had to be mounted in tandem, and the rudder engine machinery took up much space in compartments I and II. The officers' accommodation and their provisions were on the decks above this.

There were three powerful leakage pump groups, the forward, mid and aft groups, and there were two large drainage pipes running down each side of the ship. However, these were wrecked forward of frame 249 so that the forward group was unable to keep the bows from flooding. The forward group finally failed and the remaining pumps were unable to stem the massive ingress of water. Flak guns are shown here as they were planned but were never fitted.

See plate for further details.

E: SMS *SEYDLITZ*

Seydlitz was a further improvement on the *Moltke* class, the most conspicuous feature being the raised forecastle, which improved seaworthiness. The armour thickness was also improved, but the number and calibre of guns remained as before at a time when the calibre should have been increased to 30.5cm, or even better 35cm. An extra boiler room was added that housed three more boilers giving a slight improvement in speed. The division of the hull into 17 watertight compartments meant high survivability even after absorbing hits of the highest calibre shells from enemy battleships.

F: *LÜTZOW* IN THE SKAGERRAK BATTLE

SMS *Lützow* under heavy fire during the battle, already far down by the bows. There are some heavy calibre shell hits on the port side armoured belt and many in and on the forecastle. To port aft the torpedo net has been dislodged and sags. The aft funnel is painted red as a recognition device. When going on active operations the aft funnels of the ships were painted red once out of sight of land, and were repainted grey before returning within sight of land. The turrets are still trained hard aft to port, having just engaged and destroyed HMS *Invincible* on that bearing. The flag signal 'Anna' on the foremast calls the *Torpedoboot G39* alongside aft to transfer Vizeadmiral Hipper to another ship. When Vizeadmiral Hipper and *Lützow*'s Commander, Kapitän zur See Harder, parted it was with the traditional hunters call, 'Hail the Forrester!' Vizeadmiral Hipper also gave KzS Harder permission to scuttle his ship if the damage became unmanageable.

Whether through good management or good luck, the British warships obtained a remarkable number of artillery hits in the forecastles of the German battlecruisers at the Skagerrak Battle. These hits produced tremendous damage above and below the waterlines of the German ships and resulted in extensive flooding. Matrose (seaman) Fritz Loose described the hits in the forecastle of SMS *Lützow* thus: 'The forecastle, the fore part of the ship, was rent apart by several hits and showed holes which a railway locomotive could comfortably have driven through.'

The crew of *Seydlitz* had had a dress rehearsal for shell strikes with the mine hit of 24 April, and therefore were well trained and practised in damage control. Aboard *Lützow* the damage was far more extensive. Furthermore the forward leak pump group, drainage pumps normally used to pump out the flooded areas, had been disabled by a hit. Therefore the midships pump group attempted to stem the tide. Damage to *Derfflinger* was less extensive. Counter-flooding was accomplished aboard *Seydlitz*, whilst the flooding of magazines C and D on *Derfflinger* achieved the same effect. On *Lützow* the forward diesel dynamo switch room remained watertight, just as a caisson. Tragically, the flooding in the forecastle was so rapid that six men were trapped there. In a letter dated 8 June an unnamed officer wrote: 'They sat in the forward diesel dynamo room, just as a diving bell, and could not get out. They had called me once, as I had a connection with them, and reported that the water was slowly rising in their room. It was held by pumps at a certain height. They maintained courage and optimism until the last.' On *Seydlitz*

ABOVE *Lützow* moored to a buoy in Kiel. (Courtesy of Carsten Steinhorst)

BELOW **This photograph shows the result of the 12in shell hit on the conning tower of *Derfflinger* at the Skagerrak Battle. The 12in shell from *Bellerophon* caused the conning tower to vibrate violently and smoke and gases entered the tower, but otherwise the effect on the thick armour was little.**

the forward broadside torpedo room remained watertight and acted as a kind of buoyancy chamber. The final figures for flooding and the draught forward in these ships were:
Derfflinger: 3,350 tonnes; 11.5m
Seydlitz: 5,308 tonnes; 14m
Lützow: 8,319 tonnes; 17m

G: SMS *DERFFLINGER*

Derfflinger is here illustrated later in its career with a tripod mast, which carried an artillery direction position instead of just a spotting position. During the critical phases of the Skagerrak Battle the German ships were blinded by funnel and gunfire smoke and could not see their adversaries. They, however, stood out as clear targets, as the visibility favoured the British. An artillery observation position high in the mast would have been to great advantage during this difficult action. The *Derfflinger* class was already aesthetically pleasing to the eye, and the addition of the tripod mast only improved this perception.

INDEX